CLOSE ENCOUNTERS
OF THE
FATAL KIND

CLOSE ENCOUNTERS OF THE FATAL KIND

Suspicious Deaths,
Mysterious Murders,
and
Bizarre Disappearances in UFO History

By

NICK REDFERN

NEW PAGE BOOKS
A division of The Career Press, Inc.
Pompton Plains, NJ

CLOSE ENCOUNTERS OF THE FATAL KIND

EDITED BY JODI BRANDON
TYPESET BY EILEEN MUNSON
Cover illustration by John Moore
Printed in the U.S.A.

To order this title, please call toll-free 1-800-CAREER-1 (NJ and Canada: 201-848-0310) to order using VISA or MasterCard, or for further information on books from Career Press.

The Career Press, Inc.
220 West Parkway, Unit 12
Pompton Plains, NJ 07444
www.careerpress.com
www.newpagebooks.com

Library of Congress Cataloging-in-Publication Data

Redfern, Nicholas, 1964-
Close encounters of the fatal kind : suspicious deaths, mysterious murders, and bizarre disappearances in UFO history / by Nick Redfern.
    pages cm
  Includes bibliographical references and index.
  ISBN 978-1-60163-311-8 -- ISBN 978-1-60163-473-3 (ebook) 1. Human-alien encounters--History. I. Title.
  BF2050.R435 2014
  001.942--dc23

                                                      2014003197

ACKNOWLEDGMENTS

I would like to offer my very sincere thanks and deep appreciation to everyone at New Page Books and Career Press, particularly Michael Pye, Laurie Kelly-Pye, Kirsten Dalley, Kara Kumpel, Gina Schenck, Jeff Piasky, Adam Schwartz, and Jodi Brandon; and to all the staff at Warwick Associates for their fine promotion and publicity campaigns. I would also like to say a very big thank you to my literary agent, Lisa Hagan, for all her hard work and help. And major thanks to Rich Reynolds of The UFO Iconoclasts blog.

Contents

INTRODUCTION

*C*lose Encounters of the Fatal Kind is a very different book than any other that I have written on the UFO subject. It is not an examination of the UFO phenomenon itself, per se. Rather, it is a study of the many and varied people who have immersed themselves in the cosmic mystery, only to turn up stone-cold dead—sooner or later, and under deeply suspicious circumstances.

In the pages that follow you will learn of case after case of missing aircraft, vanished and dead pilots, suspiciously timed heart attacks, murders made to look like suicides, the use of mind-control techniques to provoke quick deaths, the many links between the UFO phenomenon and the November 22, 1963 assassination of President John F. Kennedy, the termination of numerous scientists with secret UFO links, journalists hung out to dry, the terrifying human equivalents of so-called cattle mutilations, and fatal illnesses provoked by close proximity to UFOs.

Immersing oneself in the world of the unidentified flying object can be exciting, illuminating, stimulating, and enlightening. That same world, however, is filled with cold-hearted killers that will not think twice about taking you out of circulation, if such action is deemed necessary. And not all of those cold-hearted killers are human....

CHAPTER 1
FROM MELTING MAN TO MAURY ISLAND

The Grim Reaper Comes Calling

I hadn't flown more than two or three minutes on my course when a bright flash reflected on my airplane. It startled me as I thought I was too close to some other aircraft. I looked every place in the sky and couldn't find where the reflection had come from until I looked to the left and the north of Mt. Rainier, where I observed a chain of nine peculiar looking aircraft flying from north to south at approximately 9,500 feet elevation and going, seemingly, in a definite direction of about 170 degrees (Palmer, 1952).

These words were made by one Kenneth Arnold, an American pilot who had an encounter with a definitive squadron of UFOs, at about 3:00 p.m. on June 24, 1947, while flying near Mount Rainier, in the Cascade Mountains (Washington). It was clear to Arnold that the craft he crossed paths with were hardly of the conventional kind:

I thought it was very peculiar that I couldn't find their tails but assumed they were some type of jet plane. The more I observed these objects, the more upset I became, as I am accustomed and familiar with most all objects flying whether I am close to the ground or at higher altitudes. The chain of these saucer-like objects [was] at least five miles long. I felt confident after I would land there would be some explanation of what I saw [sic] (Palmer, 1952).

The flying saucer was duly born.

As fascinating as the Arnold story was, and certainly still is, there is yet another early case that deserves our attention. It actually pre-dates the events of June 24, 1947, by almost a year, demonstrating that, just perhaps, the so-called modern era of Ufology did not begin with Arnold, after all. While just as fascinating as Arnold's report, it is something else, too: downright horrific. It occurred in the Brazilian village of Araçariguama and resulted in a death of beyond grisly proportions. The unfortunate victim was João Prestes Filho, a 44-year-old farmer. On the night of March 4, 1946, his life came to a shocking and nightmarish end. At the time, Filho was walking to his home in the village of Araçariguama. As he approached the village, Filho, who had spent the day fishing in the Tiete River, developed a feeling that we can all, at one time or another, relate to: that of being watched. Filho's suspicion proved to be right on target. On finally getting home, and still unable to shake off that weird sensation, Filho looked out a window and was suddenly bathed in a bright glow—or beam, his family later suggested—that emanated from some form of unknown object hovering in the dark skies above. So hot and bright was the powerful illumination, it forced Filho to mask his face and drop to the ground.

As the light suddenly went out, Filho felt his skin grow warm, then hot, and very quickly scalding. Desperate for help, he staggered around the village, pleading for someone to take away the pain. Those family members who are still alive today remember Filho exhibiting severe burns to his face and upper body. Gruesomely, by the time that Filho was taken to the nearest hospital, his body was decomposing, piece by piece—even though he was still alive, as medic Aracy Gomide confirmed in 1974. After hours of agonizing pain, Filho died, his body having literally melted away in gooey chunks in front of horrified and helpless doctors. Was it possibly the result of a terrible alien weapon? We may never know, although the reference to the unknown object in the sky is highly suggestive of a UFO component to the story. Of one thing we can be sure, however: The death of João Prestes Filho was very much an ominous sign of what was to come and what would continue up until the present day.

Death From Above

On June 21, 1947, a deeply mysterious event occurred at Maury Island (Tacoma, Washington). It is a case that, close to 70 years after it occurred, still provokes major controversy in those circles where flying saucer enthusiasts gather. And that's hardly surprising, given that it revolved around nothing less than a malfunctioning UFO that practically exploded in mid-air, the controversial deaths of a pair of military personnel, and the near-death of one of the most famous figures in the history of the UFO subject.

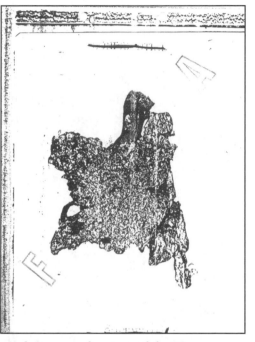

A photocopy of a piece of the Maury Island UFO debris, extracted from official FBI files (FBI 1947).

On the day in question, a man named Harold Dahl, who was under contract to salvage lumber from the Puget Sound Harbor, was out in the cold waters off Maury Island, along with half a dozen coworkers, his son, and his pet dog. Suddenly, and to their collective astonishment, they saw in the morning skies above—at a height estimated to be in the region of 2,000 feet—a squadron of what would soon become known as flying saucers, all of which displayed noticeable portholes and hollowed-out centers. Close encounters of the doughnut kind, one might be inclined to suggest. In total, they counted six craft. It was, however, the specific actions of just one of the six that really caught their collective attention.

As father, son, and crew stared upward in amazed fashion, they could not fail to see that one of the vehicles was acting in a decidedly strange way. Unlike the other saucers, this one seemed to be in trouble—*big* trouble. That became even more evident when the futuristic-looking machine plunged violently, without warning, to a height of barely 700 feet, and right above Dahl's boat. At that point, the remaining craft all descended to the same height, and one of them gently nudged, or buffeted, the malfunctioning saucer—something that made Dahl conclude it was attempting to lend some form of aerial assistance. Whatever assistance it might have been was way too little and all too late. In mere seconds, the stricken saucer evidently exploded, sending a huge amount of material crashing down from the skies. Portions of that same material—later described as falling into two distinct categories: one comprised of very thin, light-colored material of a metallic nature and the other a hot, darkly colored, slag-like substance that caused the waters to steam—slammed into Dahl's boat, injuring his son, and killing the family dog outright. The dog's death was the first in the Maury Island affair. Two more would soon be added to the list.

Amazing Stories, Alien Secrets, and a Man in Black

A thoroughly shocked, shaken, and terrified Harold Dahl quickly returned to shore. In no time at all, the story reached the ears of a man named Fred Crisman, who apparently held significant sway and influence over Dahl, and who also held a position at the harbor—although that may possibly have been a cover for work of a clandestine, intelligence-based nature. Indeed, during the Second World War, Crisman worked with the Office of Strategic Services, a forerunner of what ultimately became the Central Intelligence Agency (CIA). In the immediate post-war era Crisman was employed as an investigator for the Department of Veterans Affairs, and had links to the Atomic Energy Commission (AEC)—to the extent that specifically after the Maury Island events came to a close, he sought full-time employment with the AEC.

When told of the facts by Dahl, Crisman hastily took steps to examine the strange material for himself. By the time that Crisman reached the water's edge, the waves had already deposited much of the curious debris on the shore. It was just as Dahl had described it. Crisman wasted no time in scooping up significant portions and secreting it far away from any potentially prying eyes. And that's when an even stranger series of events unfolded—events that ultimately resulted in disaster and death.

Crisman proceeded to contact a man named Ray Palmer, the editor of *Amazing Stories* magazine, and someone with whom Crisman had previously had contact on matters of a paranormal and science-fiction nature. By the time that Palmer was fully appraised of the matter, and came to appreciate its potential enormity, the now-legendary UFO encounter of American pilot Kenneth Arnold—in the vicinity of Mount Rainier, in the Cascade Mountains—had already occurred.

Palmer, utterly excited and enthused by the story told to him by Crisman, quickly engaged Kenneth Arnold and hired him to travel to Maury Island and get to the bottom of the mystery—and as fast as possible, too. For his part, and with the controversy surrounding the flying saucer mystery spreading all across the United States, Palmer was hoping that when the facts of the Maury Island affair were finally published, they would significantly increase the sales figures of *Amazing Stories.* Palmer, as it transpires, was right on the money. Arnold quickly accepted the offer and, after flying from Boise, Idaho, was soon in Puget Sound, hot on the trail of a malfunctioning saucer, strange and unearthly debris, and Dahl and Crisman.

On his arrival, it became very apparent to Arnold that, in the immediate aftermath of the strange affair, high strangeness was afoot in and around Maury Island. It seemed that the entire locale was steeped in paranoia and fear. Dahl's life—and those of his entire family—had been threatened by what can only be described as a definitively ominous Man in Black. There was talk, and even a high degree of evidence, that many of the players in the story were being subjected to telephone bugging operations, including Arnold himself. And the military was exhibiting far more than a passing interest in the Maury Island affair, too.

As to how and why the military got involved, it went like this: When Ray Palmer hired Kenneth Arnold to look into the matter of what had gone down at Maury Island, Palmer paid him $200, a significant amount of money in 1947, just to look into a UFO report. While chatting about the Dahl-Crisman claims at the offices of the *Idaho Daily Statesman* newspaper, Arnold bragged loudly about how much he was getting paid to chase down the saucer story. This got the editor of the newspaper thinking that if Palmer was willing to shell out $200, then there had to be *something* to it. So, he sent a telegram to Air Force A-2 Intelligence to tell them what was afoot. The Maury Island mystery was about to enter a new chapter.

Murder in the Air?

It wasn't long before a pair of military men was on the scene, too: First Lieutenant Frank Mercer Brown and Captain William Lee Davidson, of Army Intelligence. Acting on the express orders of U.S. Air Force General Nathan Twining, the two were ordered to figure out what on Earth—or very possibly off it—was afoot in the waters and skies of Maury Island.

Because Arnold was in town at the expense and request of Ray Palmer, he kept the magazine editor informed of each and every development, one of which was that Crisman had handed over to Brown and Davidson certain portions of the debris collected at Puget Sound. And, the two military men were due to fly it to Wright Field, Ohio—which today is called Wright-Patterson Air Force Base, and a place where it has long been rumored UFO debris, craft, and even alien bodies have been secretly held. Unfortunately, Brown and Davidson didn't make it to Wright Field. They didn't make it to anywhere—except the grave.

Not long after Brown and Davidson took to the skies from McChord Field, their aircraft—a Boeing B-29—burst into flames, plunged to the ground, and killed both men in a fiery explosion near Kelso, Washington. The official story was that an exhaust stack on the left wing burned out, causing both the wing and its engine to catch fire, something that finally led the wing to catastrophically break off. Somewhat suspiciously, the potentially amazing debris that Crisman had given to Brown and Davidson was never retrieved from the wreckage—supposedly, at least. And there was another disturbing development, too: Arnold heard tales around town that the B-29 had been blasted out of the sky by a 20mm cannon fired by a detachment of the military that—for its own unfathomable reasons—wished to ensure the strange debris never reached Wright Field.

With Dahl by now way too frightened to talk—primarily, and understandably, as a result of his run-in with a Man in Black and the deaths of Brown and Davidson—and Crisman acting in shady and somewhat silent fashion, Arnold told Palmer that there was little more that he could do, and, as a result, he was about to head home. And, just for good measure, a United Press man, Ted Morello, warned Arnold that he (Arnold) was in way over his head, and that he should leave town at the earliest opportunity. Arnold chose to follow Morello's words, and quickly, too. It's a pity Morello didn't do likewise: He died soon after, as did one Paul Lance. The latter was a reporter for the *Tacoma Times* newspaper, a man who also reported on the incident, and who "lay on a slab in the morgue for about thirty-six hours while the pathologists hemmed and hawed" (Halbritter, 1995).

As a skilled pilot himself, Arnold flew to Maury Island, leaving his plane at a nearby airfield. On the return journey, Arnold stopped off at Pendleton, Oregon, to refuel his aircraft. Rather ominously, and perhaps far from coincidentally, after leaving Pendleton, Arnold himself experienced significant drama when his plane began to splutter and stutter. Fortunately, as a more-than-capable aviator, Arnold was able to safely bring his aircraft to the ground and to a halt, and both death and disaster were averted. It turns out that his engine had frozen in mid-air. The cause: Whoever had refueled the aircraft had left the fuel valve open. Whether by accident or design, Arnold never found out. No doubt, he preferred to conclude it was the former. Whatever really happened at Maury Island, it had already claimed two human lives. Arnold was just thankful he didn't end up as the third.

Today, and hardly surprisingly, the matter of the Maury Island affair, the deaths of First Lieutenant Frank Mercer Brown and Captain William Lee Davidson, the near-death of Kenneth Arnold, the enigmatic involvement of Fred Crisman, the deadly threats made to Harold Dahl by a

Man in Black, and the matter of that missing debris continue to perplex and puzzle. Even more so when we learn that Crisman was linked to yet another unresolved death with UFO connections—that of one of the most powerful figures of 20th-century history: President John F. Kennedy, as will become clear in a later chapter.

Chapter 2
The Victims of Roswell

Suicidal Solutions

When it comes to the matter of the infamous, UFO-themed events that occurred outside of Roswell, New Mexico, in the summer of 1947, any mention of dead bodies obviously brings to mind the stories of alleged alien corpses found on the Foster Ranch, Lincoln County, by elements of the U.S. military. But the Roswell affair, and its attendant accounts of a crashed UFO and a huge, official cover-up of the facts, provoked other fatalities, too: They are the definitively human ones. They are also the ones for whom the trauma of encountering something so shocking and strange on the desert floor plunged them into such deep states of turmoil that emotional disintegration and tragic death were the end results— *allegedly* at their own hands, but who can really say? One of those was Vern Brazel. Vern was the son of rancher Mack Brazel, who found the unusual wreckage on the ranch floor and told his story to the Roswell media—and was just 8 years old when the strange affair occurred. Unfortunately, Vern became a definitive victim of the event while still at a young age.

It is generally acknowledged by Roswell researchers that there were at least three locations on the Foster Ranch where highly strange, material evidence was found: a large debris site; a second location, where a

The Foster Ranch, the site of the Roswell, New Mexico, UFO crash of July 1947 (Nick Redfern, 2011).

significantly damaged aerial craft was found; and a third area, where a number of unusual, decaying, and badly damaged corpses were stumbled upon. Newspapers of the time reported that Vern was with his father when the latter came across the massive amount of debris strewn across the ranch. But, Vern may have seen much more than that, including the bodies. We'll never know for sure, however: No sooner as he reached an age when he could leave home, Vern said goodbye to New Mexico forever, spent a short time in the Navy before wandering around various parts of the United States, and finally, while still in his mid-20s, ending his life with a bullet to the head. On top of that, more than a few Roswell researchers have privately claimed that Mack Brazel's death, in 1963, was due to his own hand, as a result of the stress and fear provoked by encountering something so unearthly back in 1947.

Silencing the Witnesses

Then there was Dee Proctor. He was a friend of Vern Brazel who, just 7 at the time of the crash, is also acknowledged to have been involved in the discovery of anomalous items on the ranch, perhaps even alien corpses—or, as Proctor's highly protective mother, Loretta, once guardedly and tactfully referred to them, "something else" (Carey and Schmitt, 1999).

Within Roswell research, there is a belief that Dee, who used to help Mack Brazel on the ranch, even at a *very* young age, was present when

Brazel made the shocking discovery of one or more unusual, decomposing bodies on the property. That young Proctor was outrageously threatened by the military after the event, and warned not to talk about what he had seen, is not in doubt. It was a trauma-filled, life-changing experience that affected and determined the rest of Dee Proctor's existence: He died well before his time, the combined results of severe alcoholism and an out-of-control eating disorder.

Another one who plunged himself into a world dominated by alcohol was retired Major Jesse Marcel. He was the base intelligence officer at Roswell who helped to recover at least some of the debris from the site, and who became the ill-fated fall guy in the government's operation to keep everything under wraps by claiming that what was found was nothing stranger than weather balloon wreckage. Marcel's son, Jesse, Jr., acknowledged his father's severe drinking problem in the wake of the crash—and that of Jesse Jr.'s mother, too. Though the major was finally able to bring himself back from the brink of disaster, not everyone was quite so lucky. Elroy John Center, a chemist with the Battelle Memorial Institute and a man who is believed to have secretly studied the debris found at Roswell, ended his days in a sanitarium, utterly obsessed by UFOs, addicted to booze, and a shell of his former self.

Then there is the matter of Glenn Dennis, a young mortician at Ballard's Funeral Home in Roswell in 1947, who claims that, right after the crash, he received a strange telephone call from the mortuary officer at the base, during which questions were asked about the availability of child-sized caskets that could be sealed hermetically. Dennis also signed a sworn affidavit, confirming that a nurse friend at the base had admitted to him that a preliminary autopsy of the bodies had been conducted at Roswell Army Air Field. So the story went, Dennis's nurse entered one particular room to collect some supplies when she ran into a pair of doctors who were handling a gurney and three small, humanoid bodies of a very strange appearance. Two of the bodies were very badly damaged, as if wild animals had attacked and gnawed on them. Their heads were large, and their mouths were mere slits. Human, they were not, the nurse quickly came to believe.

A great deal of debate has raged for years about the veracity—or otherwise—of Dennis's tale and his nurse who no one can find or identify. This is not surprising, however, given that Dennis admitted to obfuscating time and again on her real name, preferring instead to give her a degree of anonymity. Quite understandably, this has given rise to the theory that Dennis simply created his tale. There is, however, data that strongly points in a very different direction. For example, L.M. Hall, a former chief of police in Roswell, has gone on the record as stating that Dennis told him the story of the caskets right at the time it occurred, in 1947. Similarly, Sergeant Milton Sprouse, who served at the Roswell Army Air Field in 1947, has also publicly confirmed that he heard Dennis's story decades ago. So, if the account does have merit, who really was the nurse?

The most likely candidate is Miriam Bush, who was not a nurse but an executive secretary at the base hospital in July 1947, working under the chief medical officer, Lieutenant Colonel Harold Warne. Bush's surviving family has admitted, rather notably, that, in the summer of 1947, she described to her parents the horror of seeing a number of small, humanoid bodies in a particular room at the hospital. Unfortunately, we're unable to get vindication for the story from Bush herself. In the final days of 1989, long-time-alcoholic Bush killed herself. Or did she? Pat Bush, who was married to Miriam's brother, George, has told a revealing story. Stating that Miriam Bush was "frightened her whole life long" over what she saw at the hospital on that terrible day, Pat Bush notes that her sister-in-law's death was possibly not what it seemed to be. It was far worse ("Miriam Bush," 2010).

According to Pat, just before her death Miriam checked into a hotel room, but rather curiously used her sister's name and address, instead of her own. The reason: She had become fearful that someone was watching her. Though the police stated that Miriam's death was due to suicide, Pat had major doubts that this was the case. That Miriam had bruises on her arms and a plastic bag over her head when she was found only amplified the family's suspicions. Let's not forget that Glenn Dennis went public with his story only months before Miriam Bush's dubious death. Perhaps his revelation prompted someone to have Miriam Bush removed from the equation, before she had the chance to speak openly about what she really knew about Roswell.

A Lethal Virus on the Loose

There is another aspect to the human deaths of Roswell—one that, if true, is terrifying in its implications. From the early 1990s to the final years of that decade, a UFO researcher of Big Bear Lake, California, named Timothy Cooper claimed contact with a wide and varied body of whistleblower-style figures from the world of government, the military, and the intelligence community. The Wikileaks-like group provided Cooper with literally hundreds of pages of reportedly classified documents on the Roswell incident, crashed UFOs, dead extraterrestrials, alien autopsies, and much more. That the documents exist is not in doubt. Whether they are the genuine article, or some form of disinformation designed to confuse the truth about Roswell, is a matter of keen debate. Of one thing we can be sure of, however, is that two of the documents refer to mysterious and disturbing deaths at one of the sites that have become linked to the Roswell legend. The documents in question are known as the "Interplanetary Phenomenon Unit Summary" of 1947 and the "Majestic Twelve 1st Annual Report," which is undated but believed to be of 1950s vintage.

Chronologically speaking, it is within the pages of these two documents that we begin to learn of the alleged concern exhibited by the government, military, and intelligence community in 1947 that alien beings represented a potential biological threat to the human race. Let us begin with the "Interplanetary Phenomenon Unit Summary." One section refers to shocking deaths deep in the New Mexico desert, at a site where at least some of the bodies were found: "Ground personnel from Sandia experienced some form of contamination resulting in the deaths of 3 technicians. The status of the fourth technician is unknown. Autopsies are scheduled to determine cause of death. CIC [Counter-Intelligence Corps] has made appropriate security file entries into dossiers with cross references for future review" (Wood and Wood, 1998).

On this very troubling matter, the "Majestic Twelve 1st Annual Report" expands:

> BW [biological warfare] programs in U.S. and U.K. are in
> field test stages. Discovery of new virus and bacteria agents

so lethal, that serums derived by genetic research, can launch medical science into unheard of fields of biology. The samples extracted from bodies found in New Mexico, have yielded new strains of a retro-virus not totally understood, but, give promise of the ultimate BW weapon. The danger lies in the spread of airborne and bloodborne outbreaks of diseases in large populations, with no medical cures available (Ibid.).

The document continues with respect to the reported alien technology and bodies found at the crash site:

The Panel was concerned over the contamination of several personnel upon coming in contact with debris near the power plant. One technician was overcome and collapsed when he attempted the removal of a body. Another medical technician went into a coma four hours after placing a body in a rubber body-bag. All four were rushed to Los Alamos for observation. All four later died of seizures and profuse bleeding. All four were wearing protective suits when they came into contact with body fluids from the occupants (Ibid.).

Further data was elaborated upon: "Autopsies on the four dead SED technicians are not conclusive. It is believed that the four may have suffered from some form of toxin or a highly contagious disease" (Ibid.).

Of possible connection to all this, while being interrogated by the military over his find at the Foster Ranch (to call it an interview would be way too charitable, given the trauma he was put through), Brazel was stripped bare, and given a close and careful physical examination. We might speculate that this was done to determine if the rancher was displaying any physical signs of infection—but from what?

The very idea that a fast-acting, lethal toxin, virus, or plague of alien origins was unleashed in Lincoln County, New Mexico, in the summer of 1947 sounds like the stuff of nightmares, or the script of a conspiracy-fueled science-fiction drama. Incredibly, however, the scenario receives far more than a passing degree of support from official documents that did not surface publicly until around 10 years *after* Timothy Cooper's final stash of allegedly purloined papers appeared.

New Mexico Becomes Deadly

In April 2006, the FBI declassified into the public domain—via the terms of the Freedom of Information Act—portions of a fascinating and illuminating document titled "Bacteriological Warfare in the United States" that, chiefly, covers the late 1940s to 1950, which is arguably one of the most significant periods in UFO history. Notably, of the file's original 1,783 pages, no less than 1,074 have been firmly withheld from declassification by the FBI. The reason: national security.

Nevertheless, the 709 pages that *have* been released into the public domain by the FBI have proven to be extremely valuable in helping to determine: the full scale of the link between UFO crashes in New Mexico in 1947 and alien viruses; the extent to which biological and bacteriological warfare were considered matters of extreme concern from a national security perspective in the late 1940s; and the intense secrecy that surrounded the subject at an official level during the time period at issue. More significantly, the FBI file provides strong, persuasive corroboration for certain, key data contained within the pages of several of the documents leaked to investigator Timothy Cooper in the 1990s.

Truly extraordinary, officially declassified documentation exists to show that the FBI was highly concerned by suspicious outbreaks of exotic viruses and diseases in the specific state of New Mexico in the late 1940s—and specifically in none other than Lincoln County, where the legendary UFO crash occurred. Of great significance is the fact that one of the cases the FBI examined, which is described in a heavily redacted memo of May 29, 1950, dealt with a summer 1947 outbreak of plague at a highly sensitive New Mexico installation—the Sandia Base, which played a significant role in the research and development of the atomic bomb.

As we have seen, the technicians who supposedly died when confronted by non-human bodies at one of the Roswell sites allegedly came from Sandia. On top of that, as the FBI's official papers demonstrate, the curious outbreak of plague at the base was viewed in some quarters as being the result of nothing less than a deliberate attempt to clandestinely introduce widespread contagion on the Sandia base by hostile, unknown sources.

Notably, according to yet another of the so-called leaked documents, one dated November 18, 1952, on December 6, 1950, a UFO

> impacted the earth at high speed in the Eel Indio-Guerrero area of the Texas-Mexican border after following a long trajectory through the atmosphere. By the time a search team arrived, what remains of the object had been almost totally incinerated. Such material as could be recovered was transported to the A.E.C. [Atomic Energy Commission] facility at Sandia, New Mexico, for study (Wood and Wood, 1998).

How curious that in the very same year that crashed UFO debris was reportedly transferred to Sandia, an attempt was made—by forces unidentified—to devastate the base via the introduction of an unconventional biological warfare agent. That this may have been due to the clandestine activities of visiting aliens, who had already—directly or indirectly—killed a number of technicians present at the crash site of a UFO in New Mexico, via a lethal agent, may not be as extreme as it sounds, after all.

Something of a biological warfare nature, it must be concluded, had occurred in New Mexico that subsequently led the FBI to devote countless agents, manpower, and expertise toward resolving what was taking place deep within the heart of the state. And the FBI's concern only continued. As a perfect example of this ongoing concern, consider the following— of September 1949, extracted from the "Bacteriological Warfare in the United States" document:

> Possibly some of you saw headlines in newspapers published in the States during August, such as, "Black Death Stirs Albuquerque," "Black Plague Hits Two in New Mexico," and "Dark Age Plague Found in Two." It is unfortunate that we must still seriously discuss plague, for we already know so much about its cause and mode of spread; but as long as such headlines do occur, it is necessary that we who are interested in Public Health and Preventive Medicine

do seriously consider plague and acquaint ourselves with the plague of today, its prevalence, and its potentialities (Federal Bureau of Investigation, 1950).

Again, the FBI's emphasis was on the outbreak of exotic diseases in New Mexico during the late 1940s, as the following extract from the report follows. It quotes the words of the director of the New Mexico State Public Health Laboratory, who had prepared a report on sudden and suspicious eruptions of plague in the Land of Enchantment state: "Late on August 1, 1949, the pathologist at the Veteran's Hospital in Albuquerque called stating that a man from Placitas, Sandoval County, had been admitted to the hospital and his clinical symptoms resembled plague" (Ibid.).

Lincoln County: Ground Zero

The director noted that more than a few additional cases from New Mexico had been reported in 1949, all suggestive of some form of plague on the loose. He also informed the FBI:

Since this report was written, a 7 1/2-year-old boy in Lincoln County died, possibly of plague. The boy was taken to a physician at Fort Stanton, November 4. Apparently he was not in a very serious condition and was sent home. He was returned to the Fort Stanton Hospital November 5 in the morning; his temperature was somewhat higher; by noon he was markedly worse, and by 2:30 he was dead. A post mortem examination was made and the doctor in charge diagnosed the case as being bubonic plague with pneumonic and septicemic [sic] complications (Ibid.).

There are two points with respect to this particular document that are of profound importance. First, Lincoln County, where the young boy lived and apparently contracted plague, was also the exact location of the Foster Ranch, where William Brazel stumbled upon crashed UFO debris in July 1947—a finding that quickly opened the floodgates on the Roswell controversy.

Second, that the young boy was taken to Fort Stanton is equally intriguing. On this matter, consider the words of UFO researcher Martin Cannon:

"Coincidentally" or otherwise, the Brazel ranch is located quite near Fort Stanton Mesa.... During World War II, soldiers suffering from combat fatigue and other psychological ailments were remanded there. Researcher Kathy Kasten visited Fort Stanton Mesa, and toured the facility's cemetery. She noted with great interest the sharp increase in deaths in the 1947–51 period (Cannon).

Equally intriguing is the fact that the FBI also—in this *same* period—began to carefully collect and review New Mexico–based newspaper articles on the sudden surfacing of serious, and sometimes mystifying, deadly diseases within the state. A perfect example is an article that the FBI culled from the *Albuquerque Journal* on June 21, 1950, that referred to a then-recent two-day conference held at the Atlanta, Georgia–based Communicable Disease Center "with public health workers who are conducting a survey on the plague problem in New Mexico" (Federal Bureau of Investigation, 1950).

Why the FBI was collating all of this data in a Top Secret collection of June 22, 1950 titled "Bacteriological Warfare—Espionage-Sabotage (Bubonic Plague)" is a mystery. Even more of a mystery is the highly illuminating fact that—as FBI documentation demonstrates—*all* of the previously mentioned data collected by the FBI on sudden outbreaks of plague in New Mexico, as well as the information on the death at Fort Stanton (just a short journey to the Foster Ranch) was copied to (a) the director of naval intelligence, (b) the Air Force's director of special investigations, (c) the acting director of the Division of Security of the Atomic Energy Commission, and (d) none other than the director of the CIA.

Needless to say, the likelihood that such illustrious and high-ranking individuals would have normally displayed *any* interest in human deaths inadvertently caused by disease in New Mexico seems highly unlikely, unless, as seems to be the case, national security was linked to—or was *suspected* of being linked to—the New Mexican deaths.

Roswell, it seems, may not just be the most famous of all UFO cases. It may have been the deadliest UFO case, too.

Chapter 3
Zapped by a UFO?

From Interception to Destruction

It's an incident that has very much polarized the UFO research community, in terms of what actually happened, to the point where it still remains unresolved in the minds of many. It's the strange saga of U.S. Air Force pilot Captain Thomas P. Mantell, who lost his life in 1948 while chasing a UFO high in the skies of Kentucky—or while pursuing a balloon or Venus. Take your pick. The theories are several. The facts, aside from the exact nature of what Mantell encountered, are relatively straightforward.

It all began in the early afternoon of January 7, 1948, when staff at the Kentucky-based Godman Army Air Field—a portion of Fort Knox—noticed something that, to them at least, was perceived as deeply strange: a highly reflective, circular-shaped object seemingly hovering in the skies and in disturbingly close proximity to the base. It was reportedly enormous, too. Control-tower employees at Fort Knox, the resident intelligence officer, the base commander (Colonel Guy Hix), and various high-ranking personnel did their utmost to identify the mysterious visitor. They all failed to do so, despite keeping a careful eye on it for about one and a half hours. Given that UFOs had been big news for around seven months—ever since Kenneth Arnold, in June 1947, had his celebrated flying saucer encounter over Washington State—an air of definitive unease quickly developed among those who were carefully watching the object.

As luck would have it, while Godman Army Air Field was in a state of concern, there was light on the horizon. Or, rather, there was a squadron of four P51 *Mustang* aircraft on the horizon, commanded by Captain Thomas Mantell. As Mantell's team approached Godman, they were ordered to try and identify the mystifying, hovering thing in the sky. You would imagine that four crews would have had no problem in doing exactly that. There *was* a problem, however: In almost lightning speed, those four aircraft became just one. One of the planes was severely low on fuel, something that necessitated a hasty landing at Godman Field. A second pilot, concerned over becoming somewhat disoriented due to a lack of an oxygen mask, requested permission to break off and land. Permission was granted. Such was the level of concern that the pilot had, however, a decision was taken to have the third plane escort him to the ground. In a matter of mere minutes, Mantell was, rather astonishingly, all alone, the only one left to check out the enigma in the skies. It was to be Mantell's last task as a pilot of the U.S. Air Force. It would also be the last thing he would do, period—aside, that is, from dying violently.

The P51 Mustang, *the aircraft in which Captain Thomas Mantell was killed while pursuing a UFO in 1948 (U.S. Army Airforce, 1944).*

At around 15,000 feet, Mantell—who also lacked an oxygen mask—radioed Godman to let them know he could see the object pretty clearly and added that it seemed to be moving at roughly 50 percent of his own speed, which would have put it at around 180 mph. The UFO was, Mantell added, huge in size. He ultimately climbed to around 25,000 feet, advising ground personnel that he was going to attempt a closer look. No word was ever heard from Mantell again. The unknown object vanished and, more than 120 miles from Godman, Mantell's *Mustang* ceased its climb—due to the rigors of very high-altitude exposure—and soon began to hurtle back to earth, slamming into farmland with full, pulverizing force. Mantell was, unsurprisingly, killed instantly. The official cause of the tragedy: Mantell passed out as a result of a lack of sufficient oxygen and never came to. He was just 25 years of age. Was Mantell a victim of his own carelessness and over-enthusiasm, or was his death a case of termination at the hands of lethal extraterrestrials?

Mantell's Death: Theories Abound

It's unfair, and incorrect, to put the blame on Mantell's lack of professionalism for what happened. He may have only been 25, but he was a man with thousands of air hours to his credit and someone who was decorated for his bravery in the Second World War. Clearly Mantell saw something, but what was it? It's difficult to say with 100 percent certainty, because, rather oddly, within 30 minutes of the crash, the object was gone, despite having hung in the skies for several hours previously. An investigation was clearly warranted.

That investigation fell to the U.S. Air Force's official UFO study program, Project Sign. The official verdict, at first at least, was that Mantell had misperceived the planet Venus, assuming it to have been a smaller-sized object at relatively close quarters, rather than a huge heavenly body at a multi-million-mile distance. The theory did have some merit, as Venus was in the general position to be seen. The problem, however, was that on a January afternoon, it would have been practically impossible to see the planet at all. There was another possibility—one shrouded in official, military secrecy.

At the time when UFOs were all the rage, the U.S. Navy's Office of Naval Research had developed, and was flying, very large balloons under the cover of an operation called Project Skyhook. Although chiefly utilized to collect meteorological data, Skyhooks and the attendant project were deeply classified. As for their appearance, they were very reflective, just like the unknown object seen by Mantell. Moreover, it's most unlikely that Mantell would have had an awareness of Project Skyhook, as he had no particular need to know of its existence. And there's another matter: Because Skyhook *was* such a secret project, it's not impossible that Project Sign staff found themselves in a deep quandary. If they suspected that a Skyhook balloon was the culprit, revealing such would potentially have compromised a classified operation, something that may have led to the initial promotion of the Venus theory instead. In that sense, there truly may have been a cover-up behind Mantell's death, but not because of a direct flying saucer–themed angle to the affair. There is, however, a problem with the Skyhook theory.

In 1952, the Mantell affair once again fell under official scrutiny. The investigating officer was Captain Edward Ruppelt, then the head of Project Blue Book, the Air Force's successor to Project Sign and a short-lived operation, Project Grudge, which Ruppelt also worked on. Ruppelt certainly didn't rule out the balloon theory; to him, it made a great deal of sense. Try as he might, however, Ruppelt, with all of his door-opening abilities, was unable to uncover any documentation conclusively proving that the whole thing was provoked by a disastrous case of mistaken identity.

And Ruppelt had more than a few choice words of criticism to say about the Air Force's conclusions on the encounter and subsequent death of Captain Mantell: "To use a trite term, it was a masterpiece in the art of 'weasel-wording.' It said that the UFO might have been Venus or it could have been a balloon. Maybe two balloons. It probably was Venus except that this is doubtful because Venus was too dim to be seen in the afternoon" (Ruppelt, 1956).

Captain Edward Ruppelt died, in 1960, of a heart attack at the *very* young age of 37. We will return to the matter of potentially suspicious deaths from heart disease in later chapters.

The Whistleblowers Speak

On the matter of fatal aircraft crashes in the 1940s, and specifically with UFO connections, it's worth noting the words of retired Sergeant Rita Hill of the British Royal Air Force. She spent much of her late-1940s military career at an RAF base in the English county of Wiltshire called Boscombe Down, from where—both then and now—new and radically designed experimental aircraft are test-flown. In 1998 Hill told me something that should be kept in mind when we consider the circumstances surrounding the death of Captain Mantell:

> With UFOs, I'll tell you what I can—but it was all top secret at the time. When the test-pilots had finished their tests, they would have briefings, which we would sometimes attend. These were all very hush-hush. Sometimes, the pilots would report seeing strange lights and objects in the sky. They weren't called UFOs at that time. But they would say that when they saw these strange lights, the instruments on the aircraft would go haywire and sometimes the altimeter would just stop, which is a disaster in itself (Redfern, 1998).

Hill continued:

> There were always crashes with experimental aircraft. These weren't little biplanes; we're talking about jets and so on. At times we would have a crash a week. I was in charge of a crash crew and had two lads with me. When we went to a crash site, everything had to be found—buttons off the tunics, scraps and so on. Sometimes it would take us weeks to find everything. And from there the wreckage would be taken for reconstruction. In these cases, the reports went to the Air Ministry at Whitehall [London] and we were all sworn to secrecy. It's only now that I've said anything about what I saw (Ibid.).

And there is still more testimony to come.

One man with intimate knowledge of the death of Captain Thomas Mantell was Captain James F. Duesler, the deputy commander at Godman

Air Force Base on the day that Mantell lost his life. Duesler's testimony is highly important, as he was one of the firsthand witnesses to the unusual object in the sky. He likened its shape to that of an ice-cream cone standing on its head. Not only that, there seemed to be a black-colored band around the object, one that was rotating incredibly fast. Its lower section was red in color—something that is at deep variance with the description of a Skyhook balloon.

Rather significantly, Duesler said that less than 12 hours after Mantell's death, yet another UFO was seen at Godman: It was about 1:00 a.m. the next day when a missile-shaped craft, of unknown origins and giving off an orange glow, was seen moving in a wide arc around the base. The matter was never resolved.

Then there are the comments that Duesler made about Mantell's body. Despite the fact that the aircraft had plummeted to the ground from a height of tens of thousands of feet, and although each and every one of his bones were utterly shattered, there was not even a cut or a scratch on Mantell's skin. The aircraft was not at all badly damaged—although the wings had broken off the aircraft on impact—and, in Duesler's view, was not at all consistent with what one would expect to see in an aircraft that had hit the ground with both speed and force.

So, what was it consistent with? That's a question everyone involved in this affair would sorely like answered. Venus, a secret balloon, or a genuine UFO, the jury remains steadfastly undecided.

CHAPTER 4

SILENCED ON THE 16TH FLOOR

Leaping to Conclusions

It was at 1:50 a.m. on May 22, 1949, when the life of one of the most significant figures in the history of the U.S. government came to a crashing end—and, yes, that *should* be interpreted in literal fashion. The battered body of James Forrestal, who had the honor of being the first U.S. secretary of defense, was found lying on a third-floor canopy of the Maryland-based Bethesda Naval Hospital. Forrestal had reportedly flung himself out of a window on the 16th floor. Death, after falling for 13 floors, it scarcely needs mentioning, was immediate.

It might seem logical to assume that Forrestal took his own life. After all, it's a matter of record that he was severely depressed at the time, was deeply bothered by the burden of a mountain of government secrets, and was heavily medicated for severe anxiety. Such an assumption may, however, be miles off course. Forrestal's death might have been nothing less than a case of cold-hearted murder, something prompted by fears that the secretary of defense was on the verge of revealing to the world what he secretly knew about the UFO phenomenon. But, before we get to that thorny matter of all things extraterrestrial, let's take a look at what we know for sure about the man and his untimely passing.

James Vincent Forrestal was born in Dutchess County, New York, in 1892 and, after leaving Princeton University, found employment with

William A. Read & Co., a powerful force on Wall Street. Thanks to his skills in the fields of banking and investment, Forrestal soon secured a sizeable amount of money. In 1926, when he was 34, Forrestal married Josephine Ogden, who was a senior writer for *Vogue.* The marriage was a difficult one, given that both Ogden and Forrestal had emotional issues: She suffered from violent mood swings and had a major alcohol addiction, and he found it difficult to get close to people and had even more difficultly in showing his feelings.

U.S. Secretary of Defense James Forrestal, who died under controversial circumstances, in 1949 (U.S. Government, 1940s).

In 1940, Forrestal secured a position with the U.S. government and, in an impressively short period, was offered the job of under-secretary of the Navy. He did not waste any time at all in accepting the lucrative job. Within just a few years, Forrestal rose to the rank of full secretary of the Navy. Then, in 1947, and in conjunction with the historic passing of the National Security Act, Forrestal was made first secretary of defense, by then-President Harry S. Truman. It was not long, however, before the undeniable pressures of such a prestigious but responsibility-filled job began to take their ultimately fatal toll on the man himself.

Depression soon took an unrelenting grip on Forrestal and, in 1949, amid official concerns that he was becoming unstable, erratic, and even a risk to U.S. national security, he was stripped of his position as secretary of defense. Forrestal's voluminous diaries, which ran to *thousands* of pages—and many of which still remain outside of the public domain to this very day—were handed over to the White House for what was described as safekeeping. Finally, and most certainly against his own volition, Forrestal was admitted to the Bethesda Naval Hospital for what was said to be his own safety and own good. The rest, as the old saying goes, is history. Or is it? It all depends on whose version of history you believe to be the truth.

The Countdown to the End

Prior to being admitted to Bethesda, on April 2, 1949, Forrestal feared he was being watched by shadowy sources, but whether foreign or domestic he wasn't sure. Maybe, even, it was both. He developed a significant degree of paranoia as he began to see spying eyes in all quarters. Perhaps agents of the Soviet KGB were following him, in an effort to learn certain high-level secrets of the U.S. government. On the other hand, maybe it was the FBI, keeping a clandestine watch to ensure Forrestal didn't crack up and start spewing classified data here, there, and just about everywhere. Whatever the truth, Forrestal's paranoia was not unfounded: He really was being watched—and watched *closely*—before his controversial death.

When Forrestal was committed to Bethesda he was placed in what amounted to solitary confinement in a room with heavily screened windows. When he asked the reason for the screens, Bethesda's chief psychiatrist, Captain George N. Raines, told him, in no uncertain terms that it was to keep Forrestal from jumping out the windows. Rather interestingly, given what happened to Forrestal on May 22, he replied to Raines, in almost appalled fashion, that he couldn't even begin to imagine committing suicide by jumping to his death.

Although there is no doubt that Forrestal was indeed in a fraught psychological state when he entered Bethesda (he even tried to throw himself out of the car that took him to the hospital), by all accounts his condition significantly improved over the course of the following few weeks. Only two days before his death, Forrestal was seen happily chatting with Bethesda's commanding officer, Rear Admiral Morton Willcutts. Forrestal was lucid and freshly showered, and had a healthy appetite, as evidenced by the large steak he devoured in Willcutts's company. Everything was progressing nicely—that is, until only two days later when death put in an appearance. It's also when things got decidedly murky and mysterious.

The officially accepted version of events is that Forrestal, in the hours leading up to the fatal moment, was in his room, under the watchful eye of one Edward Prise, a U.S. Navy corpsman with whom Forrestal got along very well. Forrestal reportedly told Prise that he didn't want a sedative that night, as he intended to read for a while. After Prise's shift was over (at midnight), Robert Wayne Harrison, Jr., took his place and kept watch over the secretary of defense. Or, at least, for a while he did that. At some point, Harrison, Jr., exited the room to run an errand, at which point the countdown to Forrestal's death started ticking. It got louder and louder by the minute. While in the room, and presumably on his own, an utterly distraught Forrestal tied one end of the cord of his dressing gown to the room's radiator, which was directly below the room's window, and tied the other end around his neck. He then simply climbed out of the window and, after the cord gave way under his weight, plummeted to his death, rather than dying by hanging, which may have been his original plan—if, of course, one accepts the suicide theory. There are, however, a number of reasons why we should *not* necessarily embrace the notion that Forrestal took his own life or, even, embrace *any* portion of this particular scenario.

Countering the Official Verdict

Not only was Forrestal's psychological state vastly improved by May 22, but he had made firm plans with Edward Prise to have him (Prise) become his personal chauffeur after his release from Bethesda. It was a position that Prise was eagerly looking forward to fulfilling, as the two had developed a good rapport and even a degree of friendship. On top of that, on the very day that Forrestal died, his brother, Henry—angry and concerned that Forrestal was essentially being held against his will—planned to travel to Bethesda to have Forrestal removed from his confines. That Henry Forrestal informed hospital staff—*in advance*—that he was going to take his brother home was, perhaps, hardly the wisest decision he could have made. If there was one time, more than any other, that someone may have wanted Forrestal dead, it was surely when it seemed likely he was due to leave Bethesda and be totally free of the Navy's careful watch and control. That Forrestal *did* die, and only hours before he was due to exit Bethesda, only heightened the suspicions that his death was not a suicide.

Second, there is the matter of why Forrestal was left alone. Indeed, we have conflicting versions of events. One suggests that it was Forrestal who ordered his guard to run the errand as a means to ensure that he (Forrestal) was left alone to commit his fatal act without anyone being present to stop him. A second scenario has the guard being called out of the room and the terrible deed having been undertaken by lethal assassins while Forrestal was alone.

Third, there is the controversial issue of the dressing gown cord found wrapped around Forrestal's neck. Remember that this was a cord designed to tie around Forrestal's *waist*. It seems highly unlikely that such a cord would have been long enough to (a) ensure that one end could be tied tightly around the radiator, (b) allow for the other end to be wrapped around Forrestal's neck, and (c) still permit enough cord to be left over so that Forrestal could climb out of the window. Related to this is the grim fact that when the outside wall was examined after Forrestal's death, there was clear evidence of scratch marks directly below the window—possibly suggesting Forrestal, in his final seconds, was struggling and fighting for his very life.

Fourth, we have the words of Henry Forrestal, who quickly became utterly convinced that his brother had been murdered. For Henry, his brother was throttled with the cord and then coldly thrown out of the window, by forces unknown, to his death. It was a belief that Henry held onto firmly for the rest of his life.

Whatever the ultimate cause of Forrestal's death, there are many reasons why the cause of his mental collapse may have been prompted by something other than UFOs. After all, Forrestal's passing occurred less than five years after the end of the Second World War, and at a time when civilization was still very much in a fraught state of flux. On top of that, having defeated the Nazis less than half a decade earlier, the world was now faced with the Soviet menace and its growing, flexing muscles. Forrestal, as secretary of defense, was overwhelmed by matters of a national security nature on a daily basis. Just one of these issues—never mind all of them combined—might have taken its toll on a man with already-documented psychological issues. What is fascinating, however, is that upon looking for data linking Forrestal with the UFO controversy, guess what? *We actually find it.*

Flying Saucers and the Secretary of Defense

When examining the many and varied complexities of James Forrestal's death, it's worth keeping in mind the time line, which offers us some unique and thought-provoking insight into the potentially UFO-connected world of the secretary of defense. On April 26, 1947, Congress passed the National Security Act. June 24, 1947 saw the unleashing of the flying saucer phenomenon onto the world, thanks to Kenneth Arnold. And just more than a week later, the notorious UFO crash outside of Roswell, New Mexico, occurred. Then, on September 17, 1947, President Harry S. Truman made the unusual demand that Forrestal be sworn in as secretary of defense *immediately.* Six days later, on September 23, Forrestal arrived for work in his new offices at the Pentagon.

September 23 also happened to be the very date upon which one of the most historic of all the many and varied official U.S. military documents on UFOs was prepared. Its author was General Nathan Twining of the Army Air Force (as it was known at the time). "The phenomenon reported is something real and not visionary or fictitious," wrote Twining in the classified document titled "AMC [Air Materiel Command] Opinion Concerning 'Flying Discs'" (Twining, 1947). Twining continued: "There are objects probably approximating the shape of a disc, of such appreciable size as to appear to be as large as man-made aircraft" (Ibid.). It is a document that makes it very clear that senior personnel in the U.S. military were convinced something decidedly strange was afoot in the skies of the United States.

Twenty-four hours later, Forrestal met with both President Truman and one Dr. Vannevar Bush, a brilliant scientist who, from 1947 to 1948, served as chairman of the Development Board of the National Military Establishment. Interestingly, a November 21, 1950 document on UFOs prepared by Wilbert B. Smith, an employee of the Canadian government's Department of Transport, noted with respect to the mysterious aerial craft crisscrossing the skies of our world at the time: "The matter is the most highly classified subject in the United States government, rating higher even than the H-bomb.... Flying Saucers exist.... Their modus operandi is unknown but concentrated effort is being made by a small group headed by *Doctor Vannevar Bush*" [author's emphasis] (Strainic, 2002).

Forrestal and the Men in Black

Incredibly, we even find a connection between Secretary of Defense Forrestal and the mystery of the notorious Men in Black. As noted in Chapter 1, a sinister MIB put in an appearance at the site of the controversial Maury Island affair of June 1947. It was an appearance that practically froze the blood of a terrified Harold Dahl. For a few years afterward, the MIB vanished back into the shadows. In the early 1950s, however, they were back in unbridled force. This was a time when the Men in Black began to be seen almost exclusively in groups of three. Not only that, they did not look like your average special agents of the FBI. Rather, the fedora-and-black-suit-wearing MIB were downright sinister and disturbing in appearance. Usually skinny and short in stature, with pale and sickly-looking skin, and wearing ill-fitting clothes, they terrorized UFO witnesses and investigators to their collective core. So, you may well ask, what does all that have to do with James Forrestal? The answer is: quite a lot, actually.

Only a few days before Forrestal was admitted to Bethesda, and as incredible as it may sound, he was personally embroiled in an MIB–style event. Aware that his friend was becoming more and more unhinged by the day—if not even by the hour—Ferdinand Eberstadt paid Forrestal a visit at the latter's home. Eberstadt (a banker, a lawyer, and the author of a groundbreaking 1945 document that helped shape American intelligence: "Task Force Report on National Security Organization") was shocked by what he found. All of the curtains and blinds were drawn. Forrestal would only speak in the tiniest whispers—convinced, he told Eberstadt, that the house was bugged. Forrestal was, he muttered to Eberstadt, under constant surveillance by shadowy forces. As evidence of this, Forrestal cautiously pulled back a blind and drew Eberstadt's attention to two badly dressed men who stood on the corner of the street. They were part of the conspiracy, said Forrestal, knowingly. And there was more high strangeness to follow.

Only seconds later, the doorbell rang. It was answered by one of Forrestal's staff and a brief exchange occurred. Eberstadt asked questions and was told by Forrestal's houseboy that the visitor was an odd-looking man who claimed to have been seeking Forrestal's support in getting the man elected as postmaster in his hometown. The man apparently left when it became clear that Forrestal would not be entertaining any visitors at all. As both Forrestal and Eberstadt watched carefully through the barely parted blinds, the curious fellow walked to the pair that Forrestal had previously identified as watching him, and the three briefly talked, after which the man who had knocked on the door boarded a trolley car for destinations unknown. For Forrestal, this was prime evidence of a conspiracy against him. Just perhaps, Forrestal was right on target.

This particularly odd affair is absolutely ripe with Men in Black–style overtones. As noted, the MIB often have unusual facial features and pale skin. Forrestal's mysterious visitor was described as being odd-looking. The MIB are often noted for wearing ill-fitting suits that often hang from their skinny bodies. That somewhat unsettling pair of characters standing on the corner of Forrestal's street was described as dressed badly. Then there is the matter of the visitor to Forrestal's home, who claimed to be looking for support from Forrestal in relation to a job position with the United States Post Office. This is a classic, and widely acknowledged, MIB tactic. Very often, the MIB try to worm their way into private residences by claiming to be census-takers, military personnel, police officers, or lost souls from out of town looking for a particular street in the area. And let's not forget that the group was a *trio*—the veritable hallmark of 1950s-era MIB.

Dennis Stacy, a long-term and well-respected figure in the field of UFO research, notes of this curious situation that, "the whole thing has the appearance of a one-act play staged for Forrestal's 'benefit'" (Stacy,

1993). Not only that, Stacy commented that the event "begins to smack of orchestration aimed at unsettling an already unstable Forrestal" (Ibid.). To be sure, and as Ufological history has shown, the Men in Black are very skilled indeed when it comes to "unsettling" people and provoking an "unstable" mindset in those they menacingly target (Ibid.).

How to Kill a Man, CIA-Style

For those who simply cannot bring themselves to believe that the death of Secretary of Defense Forrestal was in any way suspicious, it's worth noting the contents of a 1951 CIA document titled "A Study of Assassination." On May 23, 1997, the CIA declassified, via the terms of the Freedom of Information Act, about 1,400 pages of formerly classified files relative to its top secret involvement in a nation-changing coup in Guatemala in 1954. Contained within that particular collection of material was the aforementioned "A Study of Assassination" paper, which runs 19 pages, and informs CIA personnel of the most efficient ways to kill a person and make the death appear to be due to nothing stranger than an accident or suicide. Noting that "no assassination instructions should ever be written or recorded," the author of the document (whose name is excised from the released papers) focused a significant amount of time on the matter of killing someone by hurling them out of the window of a multi-storey building ("A Study of Assassination," 1951).

The paper stated:

> For secret assassination, either simple or chase, the contrived accident is the most effective technique. When successfully executed, it causes little excitement and is only casually investigated. The most efficient accident, in simple assassination, is a fall of 75 feet or more onto a hard surface. Elevator shafts, stair wells, unscreened windows and bridges will serve. Bridge falls into water are not reliable. In simple cases a private meeting with the subject may be arranged at a properly-cased location. The act may be executed by sudden, vigorous [deleted] of the ankles, tipping the subject over the edge. If the assassin immediately

sets up an outcry, playing the "horrified witness," no alibi or surreptitious withdrawal is necessary. In chase cases it will usually be necessary to stun or drug the subject before dropping him. Care is required to insure that no wound or condition not attributable to the fall is discernible after death (Ibid.).

Clearly, then, the CIA had well-planned guidelines in place to ensure that a fall from a window of a high building could be made to look like a tragic accident or a suicide, when, in reality, it was nothing of the sort. That the document was dated only two years after Forrestal's controversial fall from a 16th-floor, Washington, D.C. window only adds to the murder versus suicide controversy. Did the author of the report have Forrestal in mind when penning its contents? To be sure, it's an unsettling question to have to ask.

"The Untimely Death of Secretary Forrestal Was Deemed Necessary and Regrettable"

Adding to the controversy surrounding Forrestal's final day is a decidedly *unofficially* released document that was acquired in the 1990s by the father-son UFO research team of Dr. Robert Wood and Ryan Wood. The one-page document at issue was provided to them by Timothy Cooper. Problematic is the fact that Cooper claimed he received the document from a sympathetic government insider whose name we don't know. Although the author of the CIA's "A Study of Assassination" paper warns agency personnel that "no assassination instructions should ever be written or recorded," the author of the document acquired by the Woods from Cooper was apparently of a very different opinion ("A Study of Assassination," 1951).

Purportedly originating with a super-secret project allegedly known as Majestic 12, or MJ12—which, staffed by high-ranking military and intelligence-based personnel, supposedly made policy on the UFO issue in the post-Roswell era onward—the undated document states: "In protecting the security operations of MAJESTIC, it has been necessary to [deleted] individuals who would compromise the intelligence efforts. While distasteful [deleted] at times the use of [deleted] measures have been executed. The untimely death of Secretary Forrestal was deemed necessary and regrettable" ("Annex C Fragment").

That the document entered the public domain in a decidedly alternative fashion—namely, from Timothy Cooper's unknown source—and the fact that many students of Ufology believe the Majestic 12 story to be borne solely out of disinformation, whether by UFO researchers or by specialists within the intelligence community, only serve to darken the already-murky waters even more.

We may never know, for sure, if Secretary of Defense James Forrestal took his own life in the early hours of May 22, 1949, or if his death was due to powerful figures in government who, fearful that his breakdown might have prompted him to reveal what he knew about UFOs, decided that Forrestal simply had to go. One thing we *do* know for sure, however, is that just a few short months before he plummeted to his death from the 16th floor of the Bethesda Naval Hospital, Forrestal, in fear-filled fashion, told his good friend William O. Douglas, an associate justice of the Supreme Court: "Bill, something awful is about to happen to me." And, as we know, something awful most assuredly *did* happen (Hoopes and Brinkley, 2000).

CHAPTER 5
MURDER IN MIND

From Secret Project to Sudden Death

Four years after the May 22, 1949, controversial death of Secretary of Defense James Forrestal at the Bethesda Naval Hospital, Maryland, a chillingly and suspiciously similar death occurred in downtown Manhattan. And as was the case with the Forrestal affair, this particular victim also had ties to the UFO phenomenon. It's the strange and deadly saga of a man named Frank Olson, a chemist with the U.S. Army's Special Operations Division at the Maryland-based Camp Detrick, whose life came to a devastating halt on November 28, 1953. Known today as Fort Detrick, the installation happens to be one of the most sensitive of the United States, chiefly due to its longstanding research into the fields of biological warfare, chemical warfare, deadly viruses, and, most controversial of all, what has become known in generic terms as mind control.

In the domain of conspiracy-theorizing, mind control is a topic that attracts a wealth of interest and debate. And with good reason, too: For decades agencies of government have secretly worked to perfect exotic cocktails designed to manipulate, command, and enslave the human mind, very often with the intent of trying to create what might be termed real-life Manchurian Candidates. That, particularly in the 1950s, rules were broken

47

and lines were crossed when it came to the ethical (or, as it transpired, the largely unethical) use of so-called test subjects in such experimentation, is something that has given the domain of mind control justifiably notorious status. Within the clandestine world of the CIA—which worked very closely with staff at Camp Detrick—the most infamous of all its mind-manipulating programs was MKULTRA. Established in the early 1950s, the origins of the program are traceable back to the immediate post–Second World War era.

As evidence of the high level of security that shrouded the work of MKULTRA employees, it wasn't until about 30 years after the project was initiated that MKULTRA finally became known outside of the confines of the CIA. Such was the level of secrecy that had been applied to the program, even elected officials had been kept in the dark about its scope and aims. In 1975, however, everything changed. That's when the Rockefeller Commission and the Church Committee decided to try and figure out the full extent of what MKULTRA had been up to. Rather tellingly, in terms of the controversial nature of the operation, when the commission and the committee began to probe, the CIA's director at the time, Richard Helms, took rapid steps to have its archives expunged of any and all relevant documentation. Tens of thousands of pages were relegated to the furnace. Unbeknownst to Helms, however, many more pages survived, something that allowed for a degree of the truth to finally surface. The result was a highly detailed 1977 document titled "The Senate MK-Ultra Hearings."

The authors of this document recorded that:

> Research and development programs to find materials which could be used to alter human behavior were initiated in the late 1940s and early 1950s. These experimental programs originally included testing of drugs involving witting human subjects, and culminated in tests using unwitting, non-volunteer human subjects. These tests were designed to determine the potential effects of chemical or biological agents when used operationally against individuals unaware that they had received a drug (Senate Select Committee on Intelligence, 1977).

MKULTRA: A top-secret CIA program with UFO connections (CIA, 1953).

It was additionally noted by the committee:

> The decision to institute one of the Army's LSD field testing projects had been based, at least in part, on the finding that no long-term residual effects had ever resulted from the drug's administration. The CIA's failure to inform the Army of a death which resulted from the surreptitious administration of LSD to unwitting Americans, may well have resulted in the institution of an unnecessary and potentially lethal program (Ibid.).

The death in question was that of the aforementioned Frank Olson, a key player in the research of MKULTRA. At least, he was until November 28, 1953.

Taking a Hit and Taking a Tumble

There are two versions of what happened on the night that Frank Olson took his last breaths: the official story and the unofficial one. As for the former, it goes like this: On November 18, 10 days prior to his fatal finale, Olson traveled to Deep Creek Lake, Maryland, for a classified meeting with colleagues engaged in mind-manipulation operations. While there, Olson was clandestinely given an amount of lysergic acid diethylamide—far better known as LSD—to determine its effects on the man himself. The cold and calculated act was carried out by a man named Sidney Gottlieb, who ran the chemical division of the CIA's Technical Services Staff and who, having personally spiked a glass of Cointreau with LSD, offered it to Olson. It should be noted that this was at a time when the potential importance and relevance of psychedelic substances in the field of mind-harnessing were starting to be realized within the corridors of power, and particularly so on the part of the CIA and staff at Camp Detrick. In other words, targeting Olson was seen as wholly justified—by Gottlieb, anyway.

A few days later, Olson announced to his boss, Vincent Ruwit, that he was quitting the program. The effects of being hit had seemingly rewired Olson's brain and his conscience. Ruwit, seriously concerned about Olson's state of mind—and also worried that Olson might go public with what he knew of MKULTRA—offered to find help for Olson by referring him to a New York–based psychiatrist that worked with the CIA in a consulting fashion. The result was that the pair—along with Robert Lashbrook, the assistant chief of the CIA's chemical branch—headed off to the Big Apple, ostensibly to try and make things right with Olson.

Olson's trippy experience had clearly plunged him into a serious state dominated by paranoia, anxiety, and psychological disintegration. The recommendation was bleak: Olson should be institutionalized until such a point that he would finally, and hopefully, recover. Whether justified or not, this was, of course, wholly outrageous, given the fact that Olson would not have been rendered into such a psychological state in the first place had he not been secretly spiked with LSD by Sidney Gottlieb. Olson did not have time to make a full recovery, however: At about 2.30 a.m. on November 28, he flung himself to his death from a window in room 1018A, on the 10th floor of Manhattan's Statler Hotel—or, to be precise, that is the story officialdom earnestly hopes we accept as the truth. Now, it's time to look at the story officialdom earnestly hopes we *won't* accept as the truth.

Financial Compensation and Forensic Evidence

It's both amazing and disgusting that the Olson family remained wholly unaware of the many controversies surrounding Frank Olson's death until the 1970s—which is when the Rockefeller Commission and the Church Committee began poking around in those dark realms the CIA sorely wanted them to stay away from. Nevertheless, thanks to the work of both, not only did the CIA admit—albeit in grudging fashion—that Olson had indeed been dosed with LSD without his knowledge or per- mission, but on top of that the government agreed to pay the Olson family $750,000. That was not the end of things, however; not by a long shot. Two decades later, Olson's son, Eric, took a decidedly controversial step: He had his father's body exhumed so that it could be forensically examined by Professor James E. Starrs of George Washington University.

During the course of taking a close look at Frank Olson's corpse a remarkable discovery was made—namely, evidence that convincingly demonstrated that Olson had suffered from significant blunt-force trauma to both his head and his chest specifically *before* he fell, jumped, or was pushed out of a window on the 10th floor of the Statler Hotel. The conclu- sion was sensational and described as being very suggestive of a homicide. Hardly surprisingly, when faced with the facts, in 1996 the Manhattan district attorney initiated a homicide investigation into Olson's death. Although it failed to uncover sufficient data to bring charges, the inves- tigation left a black stain on the CIA, and led many commentators and observers to suspect that Olson's flying leap was hardly one of his own making.

There is another matter worth noting in relation to the blunt-force trauma that Olson suffered prior to his death: The CIA's "A Study of Assassination" manual (discussed in the chapter of this book on the death of Secretary of Defense James Forrestal) notes that, when whacking a target in fatal fashion, "[b]lows should be directed to the temple, the area just below and behind the ear, and the lower, rear portion of the skull. Of course, if the blow is very heavy, any portion of the skull will do" ("A Study of Assassination," 1951). Sounds like someone paid very careful attention to that manual.

The Controversy Continues

All we really know for sure, today, is that, exactly like Secretary of Defense James Forrestal, Frank Olson was a man who was exposed to high-level secrets on a daily basis, who worked deeply on matters of a national security nature, who suffered from a degree of psychological illness—but that was hardly his fault—and who met his terrible end after plummeting to his death late at night, allegedly of his own volition but almost certainly not. And also on this matter of the Forrestal parallels, it's intriguing to note that in the aftermath of Olson's death, the FBI observed astutely that it brought back memories of Secretary of Defense Forrestal's very similar death. It was also suggestive, FBI personnel noted, of the curious death of a man named Laurence Duggan, who, in December 1948, fell to the ground from an open window of his New York–based office—by accident, or so we are assured by officialdom. Surely with some significance and relevance, at the time he took his leap to the grave, Duggan, a former department of state employee who held a senior position with the agency in South America at the height of the Second World War, was being watched closely by FBI agents who had linked him to a Soviet spy ring.

That an extensive cover-up was put into place to hide the truth behind Frank Olson's death is not in doubt. At one end of the spectrum is the theory that the cover-up stemmed from fears that a deep investigation of Olson's death might have revealed to the press, the public, and the Soviets the extent of the work of MKULTRA and its allied programs—something that would have provoked major headaches for the CIA and personnel at Camp Detrick.

At the other end of the spectrum is a much darker possibility: In his deranged, LSD-saturated state, Olson was soundly beaten and then coldly thrown out of the window of room 10/8A by agents or hired hands of officialdom, concerned by the fact that Olson had made it clear he wanted out of MKULTRA and amid fears he was planning to go public with what he knew of the program—perhaps as a means to help clear his mind of some of the things he had seen and done in the name of national security. On top of that, the fact that Ruwit—who shared room 10108A with Olson—and Lashbrook consistently obfuscated on what they knew of the events concerning Olson's death has only served to increase suspicions that suicide was not the answer, nor was an accidental fall.

All of this leads us to an astonishing question: Is it possible that Frank Olson's death was provoked by his secret knowledge of (a) a UFO connection to MKULTRA; and (b) officialdom's attempts to fake flying saucer encounters via the use of sophisticated mind-altering technology? It may seem, at first glance, an unlikely scenario. The more we dig into it, however, the less and less unlikely the sensationally grim story becomes.

Aliens, Hallucinations, and Anarchy in France

Pont-Saint-Esprit is a small village in southern France that has become infamous for a terrifying series of events that occurred in August 1951. Literally hundreds of the villagers experienced nothing less than horrific hallucinations involving strange creatures, bizarre entities, and nightmarish monsters. The official explanation is that those affected had all fallen victim to ergot, a fungus that affects rye, and that can indeed cause graphic and horrific hallucinations and even death. Certainly, on this latter point, five of the villagers died before the terrifying wave ended. And although the ergot theory is a wholly rational and plausible one, there is a much more controversial angle to the case.

Frank Olson is known to have made a number of trips to France in 1950 and 1951, all of which were focused upon discussing with French intelligence personnel the growing amount of American research into psychedelics and mind-altering techniques. H.P. Albarelli, Jr., who has diligently pursued the matter of Frank Olson's death, secured a copy of a CIA document labeled as follows: "Re: Pont-Saint-Esprit and F. Olson Files. SO Span/France Operation file, inclusive Olson. Intel files. Hand carry to Belin—tell him to see to it that these are buried" (Thomson, 2010).

Clearly, this links Olson with Pont-Saint-Esprit, which strongly suggests the outbreak of wild hallucinations in the heart of the village was *not* due to something as innocent as ergot, after all. Interestingly, only three years later, in 1954, France was hit by a huge wave of strange activity in which people reported nerve-jangling encounters with unearthly beings that led many to believe an alien invasion was possibly underway. Witnesses claimed to have encountered dwarfish creatures that provoked fear, paranoia, paralysis, electric-shock-style sensations, and disorientation. Maybe that's exactly what happened. On the other hand, one might argue that this was just the next step in officialdom's program to try to figure out just how extensively the French mind could be harnessed and messed with.

An Interrupted Journey and LSD

Still on the matter of Pont-Saint-Esprit, one of those who dug very deeply into the story of what really happened back in 1951 was author and journalist John G. Fuller. In fact, Fuller wrote an entire book on the subject: *The Day of St. Anthony's Fire*, which was published in 1968. Fuller is, however, far better known for his UFO-themed 1966 book: *The Interrupted Journey*. It told of the famous, alleged alien abduction experience of Betty and Barney Hill near Indian Head, New Hampshire, in September 1961. Not only that, Fuller had a Frank Olson connection: In 1957, Fuller met in New York with an intriguing character, one Dr. Karlis Osis, who quietly told the author of classified CIA research into the field of LSD and mind manipulation.

A Latvian, the head of the New York–based Parapsychology Foundation, and someone whose secret work with U.S. officialdom brought him into contact with Sidney Gottlieb and Robert Lashbrook—both key figures in the circumstances surrounding Olson's mysterious death—Osis offered Fuller something amazing. It was nothing less than a chance to be the first journalist to gain access to the MKULTRA program and possibly even be allowed to write about it. We may never really know to what extent Fuller took up this offer, but the fact that some conspiracy theorists suggest the Betty and Barney Hill affair was, from start to finish, an MKULTRA operation, has given rise to an incredibly controversial theory: that Fuller was a witting player in helping to significantly disseminate the UFO angle of the Hill affair to hide its far more down-to-earth—but arguably more controversial—origins. And there's still more to come that places Frank Olson on the UFO stage.

ESP and UFOs

Andrija Puharich, an American of Yugoslavian extraction, worked from the latter part of the 1940s onward in a laboratory in Glen Cove, Maine—dubbed the Round Table Foundation—and became obsessed by the powers of the human mind and the possibility that the Earth was being visited by extraterrestrials. As a result, Puharich devoted his life to the study of both, as well as to numerous other matters of a paranormal nature, including past-life regression and reincarnation. Puharich was also a man with far more than a few ties to the covert worlds of the U.S. military and the intelligence community. He served at the level of captain in the U.S. Army and, from 1953 to 1955, was employed at the Edgewood, Maryland–based Army Chemical Center. Thus, it wasn't long at all before officialdom started to take note of Puharich's work. Given that the staffs of both Edgewood and Camp Detrick were following certain, similar lines of research, Olson met with Puharich more than a few times.

Alien Abduction or Sophisticated Simulation?

In the early 1950s, Frank Olson visited, on at least two occasions, a place called Horn Island, Mississippi. The purpose was to select a location where clandestine mind-control experimentation could proceed behind distinctly closed doors. Although only about 12 miles in length and less than a mile wide, Horn Island is a picturesque locale, dominated by white sands, lagoons, marshes, and an abundance of trees, birds, and animals, but hardly any people. Behind its veneer of inviting, pleasant normality, however, Horn Island is hiding a dark history.

Back in the 1940s, the U.S. military quietly undertook research on the island into the controversial fields of chemical and biological warfare. Then, at the dawning of the 1950s, the U.S. Army's chemical corps explored the possibility of using the area for similar testing, with Olson playing a presently unclear role in the program. Officially, at least, the project was cancelled, chiefly due to the fact that the landscape was— and still is—extremely windy, and there were concerns that powerful gusts could push dangerous, aerosol-based, mind-altering substances toward populated zones. Locals to the area tell a far different story, however. It's one filled with claims that just such a project *did* go ahead and maybe even still does, deep underground. It's also a story filled with tales of mind manipulation, hallucinogenic substances, and human-rights violations.

One of the common threads that run through such tales is that, from the late 1960s onward, officialdom began secretly testing—somewhere on Horn Island—a highly controversial compound with the ability to provoke wild and disturbing hallucinations. Its official title is 3-quinuclidinyl benzilate. It is far more infamously known as BZ. Having caught the attention of the U.S. Army in the late 1950s, BZ was used against North Vietnamese troops during the Vietnam War. So, what does all this have to do with UFOs?

Getting a Buzz From an Alien Encounter

In the early 1970s, when research was still afoot into the mind-altering effects of BZ (or *Buzz,* as it's appropriately known, and as a result of its psychedelic properties), there occurred barely 8 miles or so from Horn Island one of the most famous alleged alien abduction events ever reported. The victims—which is an appropriate term to use, as will now become apparent—were 42-year-old Charles Hickson and Calvin Parker, who was 19. Around 9:00 p.m. on the night of October 10, 1973, as they were having a relaxed night of fishing at the edge of the Pascagoula River, both men were plunged into the depths of an absolute nightmare.

A brightly lit, oval-shaped aerial craft, giving off a deep humming sound, loomed into view. Amazement turned to stark fear when, via an opening in the side of the craft, three humanoid entities floated across the still waters in the direction of Parker and Hickson. They were gray in color and about 5 feet in height, and had hands that resembled claws. Too petrified to move, the two men were suddenly seized by the creatures and hauled aboard the allegedly unearthly craft. Such was the level of Parker's fear that he actually fainted into a dead heap as one of the aliens took hold of him. Then followed a typical abduction scenario involving an intrusive examination of the pair by their cosmic kidnappers, after which they were unceremoniously dumped back on the riverbank. Disoriented, dazed, and confused, they finally called a local airbase, Keesler, whose staff referred them to the police. When the cops heard the tale, it wasn't long before the media got wind of it, too, and in no time at all the story was nationwide news. Hickson ultimately came to view the event from a positive perspective, lectured widely on his experience, and even wrote a book about it. Parker did not: He suffered a nervous collapse, kept his mouth firmly shut, and shunned any and all publicity for decades.

It so happens that 1973 was also the year in which the CIA's then-director, Richard Helms, ordered the destruction of just about each and every MKULTRA file in existence, although his plan of action was far less successful than he hoped it would be. It was an action prompted by fears that the media and the elected government—largely out of the loop on the nature and scope of the MKULTRA program—would get wind of what was afoot in the world of mind control. And that, most assuredly, was something Helms wanted to studiously avoid occurring.

There are rumors that among those burned and shredded files were a report on the Parker-Hickson affair of October 10, 1973, a file that told the *real* story of the "alien abduction"—namely that it was a secret operation in which both men were exposed to BZ. Or, possibly, to something even more mind-warping, and as a specific means to determine just how far it was possible to go in making people see just about whatever officialdom wanted them to see, including aliens.

There's very little doubt that, when it comes to the issues of Frank Olson, UFOs, and mind control, we see demonstrable evidence of linkages among all three. But why, specifically, should Olson have been targeted for assassination? H.P. Albarelli, Jr. suggests that Olson may very well have come to deeply regret his role in the Pont-Saint-Esprit affair, not to mention the attendant deaths and the psychological damage done to those French citizens that survived the terrifying, tumultuous situation.

If Olson did feel that he had significantly overstepped the boundaries between what was acceptable and what was downright unforgiveable, he may well have wanted to come clean, set the record straight, and clear his conscience—perhaps to the press, maybe to the police, or even to both. Faced with the possibility that doing so might have catastrophically revealed two things—the existence and scope of the government's mind-control programs, and the way in which the UFO subject was being used to test new chemical cocktails on the general public—certain powerful and conscience-free figures concluded there was only one answer to the problem: Olson had to go—as in, out of a 10th-story window.

Chapter 6
Flying Into Oblivion

Mysterious Skies

At about 9:30 a.m. on November 10, 1953, Karl Hunrath and Wilbur Wilkinson, two friends originally from Wisconsin but at the time living in California, hired a small airplane and took to the skies of Los Angeles. It was the last time either man was seen alive. It was the last time the aircraft was seen, too. Maybe they crashed shortly after takeoff and died fiery deaths. If so, where was the wreckage? Where were the bodies? No one, including the emergency services that launched a hasty search and rescue operation when it became apparent that something was awry, could find a single piece of telltale evidence of such an accident anywhere. It was almost as if Hunrath and Wilkinson had been abducted by aliens. In fact, that may have been *precisely* what happened to them.

When news of the pair's vanishing act surfaced, many of California's UFO researchers voiced their suspicions that Hunrath and Wilkinson had been whisked away to a faraway world by benevolent aliens—the so-called Space Brothers that dominated so much of the West Coast world of Ufology in the 1950s. Others researchers took a far bleaker approach to the whole thing and pondered the possibility that deadly aliens had lured the pair to their deaths somewhere in the mountains of California. Such thoughts were not at all unreasonable ones. Hunrath and Wilkinson were big players on the Los Angeles UFO scene at the time and, in the weeks and months leading up to their disappearances, were making it widely and loudly known that they had made contacts with at least two races of extra-terrestrials—via ESP, drugs, and Ouija boards, no less. But how had the two men become embroiled in the UFO controversy in the first place? The answer is a strange one.

Hunrath, Adamski, and the FBI

The deeply curious saga all began when Hunrath—a man with a vio-lent, hair-trigger temper, a dislike of women, and a flair for creating all manner of electronic gadgets and gizmos—decided to get hot on the flying saucer trail. That meant heading out to where most of the alien action was taking place: California. In late 1952, Hunrath quit his job in Wisconsin, left his rental house firmly behind, and took a one-way flight to Los Angeles. After quickly establishing new roots in L.A., Hunrath wasted no time at all in hooking up with the major UFO players in and around town. That included George Hunt Williamson, George Adamski, and George Van Tassel—three of the most famous, but undeniably controversial, UFO contactees of all time. As well as the three Georges, Hunrath also spent much time getting to know Frank Scully, the author of the very first book on crashed UFO incidents, *Behind the Flying Saucers,* which Scully cranked out in just six weeks in 1950. But, it was on January 12, 1953 that matters really began to develop.

On the morning of the day in question, Hunrath was hanging out at the home of George Adamski—on Palomar Mountain, California—along with Jerrold Baker, one of Adamski's faithful followers. Quite out of the blue, Hunrath boasted loudly that only a few days earlier he had met with a group of long-haired, human-like aliens in a desert area on the outskirts of Joshua Tree, California. Not only that, the hippy-like ETs had suppos-edly given Hunrath a fantastically advanced weapon that had the ability to destroy aircraft in flight. Rather oddly, Hunrath gave the deadly device its very own name: Bosco. Having no love for his own government, or even for his fellow citizens, Hunrath practically bellowed to Adamski that he might even test the weapon on an aircraft or several of the U.S. military, just to see how powerful it really was. An outraged and worried Adamski immediately ordered Hunrath off his property. And that's when the problems began.

Unknown to Hunrath, Adamski, and Baker, Adamski's secretary, Lucy McGinnis, overheard Hunrath's less-than-patriotic rant and was quite understandably unnerved by the whole situation. As a result, she chose to quietly phone the soon-to-be wife of Jerrold Baker, whose name was Irma, to let her know that her fiancé was mixing with distinctly disturbing company, namely Hunrath. Irma utterly freaked out when the details of the aircraft-destroying technology were outlined to her, petrified that her beloved Jerrold might be hauled off to jail by the Feds. So, Irma took her own course of action: She quickly called the FBI.

Within just a few hours, two unsmiling special agents of J. Edgar Hoover's crime-fighting agency were sitting on Adamski's couch, grilling him all about Bosco and Uncle Sam's aircraft, and specifically the potential threat the former posed to the latter. The pair told Adamski they had heard rumors that he, Adamski "had in his possession a machine which could draw 'flying saucers' and airplanes down from the sky" (Federal Bureau of Investigation, 1953). Although this was completely untrue, Adamski realized immediately that the FBI agents were actually talking about Hunrath—who, up until the bust-up earlier on that very same day that led to the FBI arriving, had been fairly chummy with Adamski for two months or so.

Hardly impressed by Adamski's tales of the alien variety, but finally satisfied that it was Hunrath, and not Adamski, that they needed to focus on, the G-Men left, but not before giving the petrified Adamski a stern order to keep away from Hunrath from now on. Adamski didn't need telling twice. His path never again crossed with that of Hunrath.

For the next few months, the FBI kept a careful, secret watch on just about every move that Hunrath made, just in case he really *was* in possession of advanced technology—whether of extraterrestrial or human origin—that could bring down military aircraft, or UFOs, in fatal fashion. Another reason for such intense surveillance of Hunrath was the fact that the FBI uncovered never-substantiated rumors that he was working for the Russians, trying to find out the truth about UFOs for Kremlin paymasters! During this same period, Hunrath convinced Wilbur Wilkinson, an old friend from Wisconsin, to join him in Los Angeles in his quest for the truth about UFOs. Given that Hunrath was very much a crazed Dr. Frankenstein–type to Wilkinson's meek and subservient Igor, it didn't take much to persuade Wilkinson to make the move, which occurred in March 1953.

Seeking Out the Saucer People

When Wilkinson and his wife reached Los Angeles, they found themselves a pleasant home, settled into their new lives, and became more and more immersed in the UFO issue. Whereas Wilkinson's wife was content to remain an interested, but somewhat detached and slightly cynical, observer of the phenomenon, Wilkinson himself became overwhelmingly obsessed by all things of a flying saucer nature. On several occasions in the months that followed, Hunrath and Wilkinson traveled to the Prescott, Arizona, home of George Hunt Williamson to further their UFO pursuits.

The three spent hours engaged in nighttime experimentation—under the stars—trying to contact extraterrestrial entities on a telepathic-style basis. Reportedly, this was achieved by taking hits of mescaline and plunging their minds into decidedly altered states. Supposedly, such experimentation worked all too well. On one particular night during the first week of November 1953, Hunrath and Wilkinson received the mind-to-mind invite from their disembodied contacts from above that ultimately relegated them to oblivion, and provoked wild rumors that the pair had been kidnapped, or even killed, by alien entities. With matters having now reached their peak, the two said their goodbyes to Williamson—who was the very last person in the flying saucer field to ever see them—and planned the final countdown to cosmic contact. As to what happened next, it's still a matter of conjecture, six decades later.

Ten days after the two disappeared, the *Los Angeles Mirror* newspaper highlighted the mystifying affair in its pages—as well as the attendant theory that their vanishing act was the work of aliens, good, evil, or indifferent. Suddenly, and hardly surprisingly, pretty much the entirety of the rest of the city's media descended upon the Wilkinson home. When the press arrived they found that the walls of Wilkinson's den were covered—from almost floor to ceiling—with photos, drawings, press clippings, and more, all on the subject of UFOs.

On top of that, what the *Los Angeles Mirror* described as strange signs and formulas—but which Mrs. Wilkinson said was actually an interplanetary language—were scrawled on numerous sheets of paper that lay in haphazard, discarded-looking fashion on the floor. When questioned about all of this, Mrs. Wilkinson stated that although she was not overly into the subject of UFOs, her husband certainly was, chiefly as a result of Hunrath's bullying encouragement. She added—in a fashion that only increased the weirdness—the two men had recently been in contact with an alien name Regga, from the planet Masar. Quite what the Los Angeles media thought of that is anyone's guess ("Saucer Investigators in Strange Disappearance," 1953).

Was it true? Were Hunrath and Wilkinson invited to take a one-way trip to another, faraway world by benevolent aliens? Or was the whole thing a fatal ruse—a terrible ploy engineered by deadly extraterrestrials, as some of their friends and family members suspected? Others speculated that the whole affair could be explained away as mere accident and offered that nothing stranger than engine trouble had probably led to terrible tragedy and death on the mountains of California. Some, however, weren't quite so sure that the baffling disappearance of Hunrath and Wilkinson was just due to careless pilot error or mechanical malfunction. But those same souls weren't looking to ET for the answers, either. They were looking across the border or to the government. And not just the U.S. government.

George Hunt Williamson, who, as we have seen, spent considerable time with Hunrath and Wilkinson, was one of the more vocal ones on this matter:

> Some people think the two men went to Mexico, but they didn't have enough fuel for the trip. It has also been reported that Karl is in England and will reappear shortly and also that he has been seen recently in Los Angeles

with his hair dyed. He has been called a spaceman, a man possessed of evil spirits, an angel, a member of the F.B.I., and a Russian spy. What he really was no-one [sic] knows (Williamson, 1953).

Despite having occurred more than 60 years ago, the story of the baffling disappearance of Hunrath and Wilkinson refuses to fully roll over and die. Shortly before his death in November 2012, at the age of 81, long-time UFO researcher Jim Moseley shared with me his decades-old notes on the Hunrath-Wilkinson affair, compiled as part of a plan to write an ultimately aborted book on the 1950s-era UFO scene.

In part, Moseley's December 1953 notes state that certain, pertinent information was brought to his attention by Manon Darlaine, a rich, elderly woman who worked with French Intelligence during the First World War and who later moved to Los Angeles to follow her passion for UFOs. In Moseley's own words, and according to Darlaine, the aircraft in which Hunrath and Wilkinson vanished "has been found, but the men have not. The plane was dismantled, i.e., taken apart carefully and willfully, but not destroyed or damaged as it would be in a crash. This fact serves to deepen the mystery" (Moseley, 1953).

It certainly does deepen the puzzle. With Darlaine, Williamson, Adamski, Hunrath, and Wilkinson all long gone, and Moseley having now passed on, too, it seems that whatever really led to the disappearance of that curious pair of UFO researchers in the November 1953 skies of California is something destined to remain a mystery.

A Plane Crashes; Two Men Die

Despite the long and winding nature of the story, and its undeniable links to the UFO phenomenon, one has to wonder if Karl Hunrath and Wilbur Wilkinson really *were* taken out of circulation by extraterrestrials or if their vanishing act was carefully staged. There's a very good reason for that speculation. It revolves around two things in particular. Recall that Hunrath was (a) originally from Racine, Wisconsin and (b) had supposedly been given an advanced alien weapon that could disable and destroy U.S. military aircraft. This was the oddly named Bosco, you will recall. Under very weird circumstances, less than two weeks after Hunrath and Wilkinson went missing, and only a short distance from Racine, two baffling and deadly events occurred, both involving military jets, one of which crashed and the other vanished, never to be seen again.

It all began on the afternoon of November 23, 1953, when a Northrop F-89 *Scorpion* aircraft, flying out of Truax Field, Madison, Wisconsin, plunged from the skies and slammed into the swampy shores of Lake Wingra, a small body of water, also in Madison. On board were pilot First Lieutenant John W. Schmidt and radar operator Captain Glen E. Collins. The story was big news for the people of Madison. It was tragic news, too, because both men were killed in the crash.

Madison's local newspaper, the *Capital Times,* on November 24, 1953, noted that one Colonel Shoup, a spokesperson for Truax Field, was "convinced that the men had stuck with their plane in an attempt to keep it from crashing into densely-occupied areas of Madison. He praised the cooperation of police, firemen, members of the press and radio and others in trying to find the men" ("Second Truax Jet, 2 Fliers Missing," 1953). The newspaper added that a "sudden mechanical failure" caused the crash—a "failure" that occurred so quickly neither Schmidt nor Collins had time to bail out or make a distress call (Ibid.). Significantly, when Major Donald E. Keyhoe—a noted UFO investigator from the 1950s to the 1980s—looked into the matter, he learned from a colleague, Frank Edwards, that "several witnesses said a saucer flew near the plane, just before it dived into a swamp" (Ibid.).

The distance from Karl Hunrath's hometown of Racine, Wisconsin, to Madison, Wisconsin, was just 104 miles by road, which would have presented no problems in transporting the allegedly shocbox-sized Bosco and deploying it somewhere in the vicinity of Madison. Two deaths were tragic enough, but the day was not yet over. The lives of yet *another* F-89 *Scorpion* crew from Truax Field would come to an end, and only hours later.

Two More Missing in Action

On the evening of November 23, 1953 (just five days before the mysterious death of MKULTRA player Frank Olson), an F-89, piloted by

First Lieutenant Felix Moncla, Jr., took to the skies from Truax Field. This was specifically in response to an alert of an unknown aircraft flying over Lake Superior, specifically in the area of the Soo Locks, a series of locks linking the lake with the rest of the Great Lakes. The alert had come from what is today Kincheloe Air Force Base (at that time named Kinross Air Force Base). Its staff wasted no time in contacting the 433rd Fighter Interception Squadron at Truax Field. In minutes, Moncla and his radar operator, Second Lieutenant Robert L. Wilson, were airborne and in determined, hot pursuit.

The official record shows that Moncla first took his aircraft to a height of around 30,000 feet, and as he closed in on his target, descended rapidly, with the intention of surprising whoever was flying the unknown craft by coming in directly from above. It didn't quite work out as Moncla had hoped, however. It didn't work out at all. Radar plots showed that as the F-89 raced toward the unidentified vehicle, at a height of around 8,000 feet, both aircraft vanished from the scopes. Yet another aircraft, from an airbase less than two hours' drive from Karl Hunrath's hometown of Racine, Wisconsin, was no more.

The Northrop F-89 Scorpion *in the skies, November 1953 (U.S. Air Force, 1950s).*

Did the F-89 collide with the unidentified intruder? If so, did the remains of both craft sink deep into the depths of Lake Superior? If so, what, exactly, had Moncla and Wilson hit? Or, was the F-89 blasted out of the skies by an intruder that quickly made its escape? Could the two men and their aircraft have been whisked away to another world by less-than-friendly extraterrestrials? We don't have the answers to those questions, unfortunately. We *do*, however, have the Air Force's Aircraft Accident Report, which offers a valuable summary of what was determined. In part, it reveals:

> Aircraft took off at 2322 Zebra 23 Nov 53 on an active Air Defense Mission to intercept an unknown aircraft approximately 160 miles Northwest of Kinross Air Force Base. The aircraft was under radar control throughout the interception. At approximately 2352 Zebra the last radio contact was made by the radar station controlling the interception. At approximately 2355 Zebra the unknown aircraft and the F-89 merged together on the radar scope. Shortly thereafter the IFF signal disappeared from the radar scope. No further contact was established with the F-89. An extensive aerial search has revealed no trace of the aircraft. The aircraft and its crew are still missing (Ploeg, 2006).

They remained missing, too, which is hardly surprising. The night temperature was less than freezing, dense snow was falling in droves, and the waters of Lake Superior were so cold that surviving in them for more than a minute or so was a near-certain impossibility. Despite the unlikely scenario of either man being found alive, in rapid time the military had aircraft in the area, dropping flares in the hope that they might illuminate their men, floating in the waters. No luck. Similarly, a search of the lake the next morning, involving dozens of boats, came back equally empty-handed.

As for the theories regarding what happened, the Air Force mused upon the idea that the so-called unknown was actually nothing stranger than a Royal Canadian Air Force C-47 aircraft in the area at the time, and that the deaths of Moncla and Wilson were caused by the former becoming disoriented via vertigo, as he sought to close in on his quarry, and ended with the aircraft plunging into the lake. The Canadian Air Force, however, flatly denied any of their aircraft could have been the cause of the fuss that ended in death—chiefly because none were in the area in the first place!

It's important to note the comments and observations of UFO investigator Richard Hall:

> Exactly what happens that night remains unclear, as the Air Force acknowledges, and serious unanswered questions remain. How likely is it that a pilot could suffer from vertigo when flying on instruments, as official records indicate was the case? If the F-89 did intercept an RCAF C-47, why did the "blip" of the C-47 also disappear off the radar scope? Why did the Air Force invoke a Canadian C-47, which RCAF spokesmen later stated was not there (Hall, 2013)?

It seems highly unlikely that one military base should have lost two aircraft, and four men, in a period of mere hours and for there not to have been a connection. That, in the first event, we have testimony of people having seen a saucer-shaped object in the direct vicinity of the ill-fated F-89, and that, in the second, the incident matters revolved around a vehicle of definitively unknown origins or intent, it's not out of the question that aliens were the culprits, as controversial as such a scenario may sound.

Or, maybe, this really was a case of Karl Hunrath having the last laugh. Perhaps he and Wilbur Wilkinson did *not* die on the mountainous terrain of California, after all. Maybe they survived, made their stealthy way to Wisconsin—where both men were from—and unleashed the awesome power of Bosco on the U.S. Air Force's finest. Whether it was all due to the work of aliens, or of two strange characters following the orders of their extraterrestrial masters, the answer remains very much to be seen.

The final words go to First Lieutenant Felix Moncla's mother, who told UFO researcher Major Donald E. Keyhoe: "I suppose the Air Force has its reasons for not letting us know, but it is sad for a mother" (Keyhoe, 1974).

CHAPTER 7
WHEN MURDER AND SUICIDE CROSS PATHS

A Fatality in the Park

At about 6:15 p.m. on the evening of April 20, 1959, John Goode, an employee of the Matheson Hammock Park, Miami, Florida, was driving around its pleasant environs, chiefly to make sure that all was fine and that no one was about to get locked in when the gates closed at 7:00 p.m. As it transpired, all was *not* fine—far from it, actually, as Goode, to his horror, was just about to find out. As he drove slowly by a designated picnic spot, Goode couldn't help but see a Chevy just sitting there, at the side of the road, somehow curiously out of place. Goode casually headed over to let the driver know it was time to leave when he noticed something that turned his stomach. The engine was running and a hosepipe was sticking out of the slightly open rear window of the vehicle, extending down to the exhaust. Wet towels surrounded the hose, clearly having been stuffed there to ensure that no amount of oxygen would get into the station wagon. Whoever had taken such a tragic option had made sure that death was going to be inevitable and quick.

A panicked Goode flung the driver's door open, but, in an instant, he could see that he was too late. Near-choking fumes spewed forth, causing

Goode to catch his breath, as he was confronted by the sight of a late-middle-aged man, sitting in the seat upright and staring vacantly ahead. It was a scene as much of eerie calm as it was shock and tragedy. Goode, doing his best to keep his wits about him, quickly contacted his supervisor, the park's manager, R.R. Penny, who equally quickly called the police. It wasn't long at all before emergency services were on the scene. With darkness falling fast, Dr. Joseph H. Davis, the Dade County medical examiner, was soon on site, too. By 8:00 p.m. it was pretty much all over: Davis and a colleague, a Dr. Shepherd, confirmed death by carbon-monoxide poisoning and the workers at the local morgue were soon destined to receive a new arrival. It was just another suicide, a life filled with misery brought to an irreversible end. Or, was there more to it than that? In fact, was there *far more* to it than that? The answer, to both questions, is yes.

From South America to a Secret Experiment

The man whose life was snuffed out on that April evening in the Matheson Hammock Park was Morris Ketchum Jessup. At the time of his death, Jessup was just 59. He left behind him a noted legacy. Born at the turn of the 20th century, Jessup had a skilled mind, and by the age of 26 had attained both a master of science and a bachelor of science, both from the University of Michigan. Though Jessup's primary goal was to work in the cutting-edge field of astrophysics, as the years progressed and as the 1950s dawned, Jessup found himself becoming more and more involved in two very different areas of research:

1. The mysteries of the distant past, such as the questions surrounding how the gigantic structures of the ancients—Stonehenge and the pyramids of Egypt being two of many examples—were constructed, and

2. The growing presence of UFOs in the world's skies.

It was research that Jessup funded by his work as a photographer, which was a big difference from his planned, but ultimately aborted, career in astrophysics.

Jessup was not content to look for the answers he sought in books. He spent months traveling across Central America, South America, and

Mexico, as he searched for the truths behind that one question that so deeply occupied his mind and time: How did ancient man manage to move and lift multi-ton stones into the air and seemingly effortlessly create such epic structures? He had an answer, and a controversial one, too:

> I have seen and touched stonework carved out of the solid mountains of rock in South America, which certainly antedate the Andean glaciers, and almost as certainly predate the formation of the mountain themselves. This work is superior in technique to that accomplished by our currently mechanized civilization. Much of that construction, sculpture and tunneling could only have been accomplished by "forces" different from those in use by us today. The quandary is largely resolvable by admitting to a levitating force (Jessup, 1955).

As for who was responsible for the astonishing technology that allowed such construction to have taken place, Jessup was adamant in his conclusion that "flying saucers used some means of reacting with the gravitational field" (Jessup, *The Expanding Case for the UFO,* 1957). He added: "In this way they could apply accelerations or lifting forces to all particles of a body, inside and outside, simultaneously, and not through external force applied by pressure, or harness, to the surface only. I believe that this same, or a similar force was used to move stones in very ancient times" (Ibid.).

Jessup's thoughts and observations were extensively detailed in his 1955 book, *The Case for the UFO.* It was a book made notable by the fact that not only were its contents groundbreaking, but it set off alarm bells within none other than the corridors of power, specifically those of the U.S. Navy.

The Case for an Investigation

Precisely why the U.S. Navy became embroiled in the matter of the life and work of Morris K. Jessup is a very strange story all in its own. Almost immediately after *The Case for the UFO* was published, Jessup received a letter, which was forwarded to him by his publisher. Another soon followed, as did a third. And, then, a fourth appeared in Jessup's mailbox. And so it went, on and on. The writer behind all the letters was one Carlos Allende, a former seaman with the U.S. Navy. As Jessup read Allende's words, he wasn't sure if he was dealing with a madman or if he had been tipped off to the story of the century. Allende's correspondence was, chiefly, on two topics: (1) Jessup's views on levitation in the ancient past, and (2) a supposed highly classified experiment undertaken by the U.S. Navy to make a warship radar invisible, but that went terribly wrong and briefly rendered the craft and crew optically invisible—something that allegedly left some of the crew members dead and others mad as hatters. It has since become infamously known as "The Philadelphia Experiment," a veritable millstone around the Navy's neck, one that, today, has mutated into an epic saga filled with tales of cover-ups and conspiracies, time-traveling sailors, and futuristic technologies.

The USS Eldridge, *which was allegedly made invisible in "The Philadelphia Experiment" (U.S. Navy, 1944).*

Unbeknownst to Jessup, two years later, in early 1957, Allende anonymously mailed a copy of *The Case for the UFO* to the U.S. Navy. It reached the heart of an Office of Naval Research (ONR) project researching fringe technologies, and new and novel weapons systems. The copy of Jessup's book in question was filled with odd, scrawled ramblings from Allende, many of them on Egyptian and South American levitation techniques, flying saucers in both past and present, and the thorny matter of that secret experiment in invisibility, which supposedly occurred in the Philadelphia

Naval Yard in 1943. One might suspect Navy staff would have tossed the book out with the garbage. They did not. Instead, they did something most curious: They invited Jessup to meet with senior personnel in Washington, D.C., to discuss his findings.

It was, for Jessup, both a positive and a taxing time. On the one hand, that officialdom was seemingly taking his book seriously made him excited and even awed. On the other hand, Jessup became deeply worried: What if the Navy's interest in *The Case for the UFO* was just a ruse? What if its *real* intention was to ferret out exactly what he (Jessup) knew about Carlos Allende—a man who, Jessup suspected, may have significantly compromised national security by releasing details of a highly secret, classified U.S. Navy project? Was Carlos Allende the Edward Snowden of the day?

Whatever the answers, Jessup became not just worried, but deeply paranoid. Though the meeting with the Navy was not a traumatic one—in fact, it was undertaken in quite relaxed fashion—the fact that Jessup's interviewees, Captain Sidney Sherby and Commander George W. Hoover (of the Office of Naval Research's Special Projects Office), spent a significant amount of time asking about Allende got Jessup in a state of deep stress. And even more so when Jessup learned that the ONR had contracted the Texas-based Varo Corporation to run off a couple of dozen copies of the Allende-annotated version of Jessup's book. As for whose eyes the books were destined? Senior Navy personnel, something else that got Jessup in a state of anxiety. One can debate forever and a day if Jessup's worries were actually warranted or not, but it's indisputable that, in the wake of the ONR meeting, his personality soon began to change, his work suffered, and his private life took a significant turn for the worse. The countdown to the fatal events of April 20, 1959, was well and truly on the cards.

Paranoia and Fear

In the aftermath of Jessup's face to face with the U.S. Navy, strange things began occurring—*very* strange things. Jessup's personal notes reveal that, at all times of the night and day, he became the victim of hang-up phone calls, of voices on the line speaking in unfathomable words, of foreign-sounding characters screaming down the phone, and of strange, static-like noises coming through the earpiece. Collectively, this all led to a worrying suspicion on Jessup's part that his phone was bugged. It must be said, too, that all of this is highly reminiscent of the destabilizing tactics of the ominous Men in Black that, since the latter part of the 1940s, have intimidated and silenced numerous people within the UFO field—allegedly, on occasion, fatally so.

Then, in late 1958, Jessup had a dinner engagement at the house of his friend and anomalies researcher Ivan T. Sanderson, who penned a number of books on UFOs and mysteries of the paranormal kind, including *Uninvited Visitors,* a detailed study of the origin and nature of the UFO phenomenon. After the dinner, a visibly worried Jessup asked Sanderson if the two of them, along with three other guests at the party, could have a private conversation in Sanderson's study. Although puzzled, and more than a little concerned by Jessup's clearly fraught and frazzled manner, Sanderson agreed.

It was during this behind-closed-doors meeting that a twitchy, brandy-gulping Jessup shakily took out of his briefcase one of the Varo Corporation's versions of his (Jessup's) very own book, *The Case for the UFO.* But, this one was slightly different to all the rest: Jessup had added his *own* annotations to those originally written in the book's pages by Carlos Allende. He handed the book to Sanderson, begging him, in whispered tones, to lock it away, in case anything should happen to him. This was, to be sure, not a good sign.

On top of that, in the months leading up to his death, Jessup was hit by a wave of very strange synchronicities—or meaningful coincidences, one might say. The world around us, Jessup came to believe, was not all it appeared to be. Neither was what we accept as reality. Worse still, shadowy forces, whether government agents, aliens, or supernatural entities bent on Jessup's destruction, were everywhere—or so Jessup believed.

And if that wasn't enough, Jessup experienced a distinct run of bad luck. After moving to Florida in late 1958 with his wife, Rubeye, Jessup was involved in a violent car crash. For the life of him, Jessup could not begin to understand how it happened, except to speculate that someone, or something, had taken control of his mental faculties and thought processes at the time. Jessup was significantly injured in the crash, spent weeks in recovery, and developed a dark obsession that he simply could not shake off: Someone wanted him gone—as in *forever*. If that wasn't bad enough, Jessup fell out of favor with his publisher, who turned down idea after idea for future books from him.

There was even more stress for Jessup: His marriage became strained, to the point where he and Rubeye parted ways, although they did not divorce; Jessup's death prevented that from happening. Something else happened, too: Jessup spoke with, and visited with, a number of friends, including UFO investigator Riley Crabb, intimating that he was thinking of taking his own life—something that Gray Barker, the author of the 1956 book *They Knew Too Much About Flying Saucers,* also confirmed. And then, finally, there was nothing, ever again—nothing except a life cut all too short in a Miami, Florida, park one evening in April 1959.

Problems With the Suicide Theory

Although it seems likely that Morris K. Jessup *did* take his own life, things aren't quite as straightforward as one might assume. First, even though suicide was the obvious and likely cause of death, Jessup's body was not subjected to an autopsy. Instead, the conclusion of suicide was based upon one thing and one thing only: It *looked* like suicide.

Then there was the matter of those wet towels that were blocking the opening in the rear-window of Jessup's Chevy. Rubeye was able to confirm that the towels were not theirs. Granted, one can never really know what goes though someone's mind when he or she decides to end it all, but Rubeye's observations *do* beg an important question: Why did Jessup seemingly go out of his way to by *new* towels, instead of simply taking with him a few old ones from the family home?

There is another possibility: Maybe the towels *weren't* put there by Jessup, but by one of those hostile figures Jessup feared were lurking around just about every corner and amid every shadow. This possibility is made all the more feasible by one thing: When Jessup's body was found by John Goode, the towels were soaking wet. Where was the container, or the bucket, that Jessup filled with water in advance, and used to soak the towels? Answer: There *was* no container; either in the car or anywhere near to it. Could Jessup have simply drenched the towels in the park's lake, thrown them onto one of the seats of his vehicle, driven to the site of his looming death, and then stuffed the towels into the window? Though that scenario is certainly not an impossible one, the waters of the lake were dark, thus making it likely that not only would the towels have been stained from the lake water, but so would the seats, or the trunk of Jessup's Chevy, had the towels been placed there. They were *not* stained, however, nor did the seats have any noticeable odor of lake water. Something didn't add up.

There was something else that didn't add up, too: The night before his death, a buoyant and excited Jessup phoned his good friend Dr. Manson Valentine, an oceanographer and archaeologist with an interest in the story of the Philadelphia Experiment and the possibility that the pyramids of South America and Egypt were constructed via levitation-based technology, to let him know that he (Jessup) had made a big breakthrough in his work and that he wanted to share his findings with Valentine the very next day. They agreed to meet for lunch—a lunch that, history and fate have shown, was destined never to be.

Although it was unsettling things like those just mentioned that led a number of Jessup's colleagues—and particularly so Dr. Manson Valentine—to strongly doubt the official verdict of suicide, the death of Morris Jessup was one that, over time, got relegated to the sidelines and largely forgotten about. Or, for a couple of decades it was largely forgotten.

New Investigations and New Discoveries

In 1977, nearly two decades after that untimely and suspicious death, matters began to heat up significantly with regard to the Jessup affair. That's when a woman named Anna Lykins Genzlinger got involved in the matter of Jessup's death. Having become interested in the story, Genzlinger, on one particular morning in 1977, telephoned Gray Barker, author, publisher, and the man behind the book *The Strange Case of Dr. M.K. Jessup,* to speak with him about the circumstances of Jessup's final day. Because Barker was himself deeply familiar with the Jessup controversy, he was the ideal person for Genzlinger to approach and state: "I *know* Jessup did not willingly take his own life" (Genzlinger, 1981). Barker tried to remain polite, but, frankly, he had heard it all before and time and time again. And he knew that, regardless of what did or did not happen, there was likely nothing new to be found—conclusive or otherwise. Barker was wrong.

Spurred on, rather than discouraged, by Barker's less-than-enthusiastic response, Genzlinger decided to go back to the beginning. She set her sights on uncovering just about all that she could on Jessup, his work, his life, and—most important of all—his death. At the same time that Genzlinger was hot on the trail of the truth, writers Charles Berlitz and William Moore were working on their book, *The Philadelphia Experiment,* which, on its publication in 1979, was destined to reveal yet more about that controversial suicide. Something was in the air, Jessup was about to become big news again, and, as a result, the always-enterprising Gray Barker saw room for a new, fresh look at the Jessup controversy. He offered Genzlinger a book deal, which she heartily accepted. *The Jessup Dimension* surfaced in 1981.

Though neither the Genzlinger book nor the Berlitz-Moore title proved conclusively that Jessup was murdered, or was somehow deliberately made to take his own life, both releases noted the significant problems with the official line, as well as the curious series of events that preceded Jessup's death, such as that odd and violent car crash, the strange phone calls, and Jessup's fear-filled conversation with Ivan Sanderson in the latter's study late one autumn night in October 1958. But if murder, or even a strangely provoked suicide, how was such achieved? To answer that question, we have to take a trip into the weird world of lethal weaponry of the truly incredible kind.

Driven to Take One's Own Life

One of the most intriguing pieces of documentation that may help to explain how, and why, Dr. Morris Jessup ended his life (or was made to end his life), is a March 1976 report titled "Biological Effects of Electromagnetic Radiation (Radiowaves and Microwaves) Eurasian Communist Countries." Prepared for the Defense Intelligence Agency by

Ronald L. Adams and Dr. R. A. Williams of the U.S. Army's Medical Intelligence and Information Agency, it tells a dark and disturbing story of how, just maybe, someone might be made to commit suicide. The 35-page report focuses on the issue of Soviet research into microwave and radio-wave technologies and the means by which they could be weaponized, chiefly to destabilize a targeted individual via the disruption of their nervous-system and mental faculties.

Adams and Williams noted in their report that: "The Eurasian Communist countries are actively involved in evaluation of the biological significance of radio-waves and microwaves. Most of the research being conducted involves animals or in vitro evaluations, but active programs of a retrospective nature designed to elucidate the effects on humans are also being conducted" (Adams and Williams, 1976).

A particularly disturbing aspect of the Soviet research, the authors of the report revealed, was the revelation that microwave technology could be utilized to make the target believe he or she was hearing voices in his or her head—in full-blown schizophrenia-style, no less. On top of that, the voices could be used to direct the same person to perform a specific task. That such a task might be to commit suicide cannot be ruled out, when we take into consideration the following statement of Adams and Williams: "Sounds and possibly even words which appear to be originating intra-cranially can be induced by signal modulation at very low average-power densities" (Ibid.).

Interestingly, the report notes that U.S. media sources had first highlighted classified research into the phenomenon of hearing voices around 1962/1963, some 13 years before the report was written. The discoveries of the media, however, suggested that such research was well underway back in the mid-1950s, and *years* before Jessup's death, thus making it not impossible that such technology was used against Jessup in the period from the time of his meeting with the Navy, in 1957, and right up until his death in April 1959. The authors of the U.S. Army's Medical Intelligence and Information Agency report offered a notable warning: "The Soviets will continue to investigate the nature of internal sound perception. Their research will include studies on perceptual distortion and other psycho-physiological effects. The results of these investigations could have military applications if the Soviets develop methods for disrupting or disturbing human behavior" (Ibid.).

Equally distressing were the emotional and psychological effects that a radio-wave or microwave-based weapon could have on the victim. The list of side effects, noted by Adams and Williams, makes for decidedly uncomfortable reading. The spinoff effects included: "...headache, fatigue, perspiring, dizziness, menstrual disorders, irritability, agitation, tension, drowsiness, sleeplessness, depression, anxiety, forgetfulness, and lack of concentration" (Ibid.). Certainly, depression, tension, anxiety, agitation, and a lack of concentration—the latter seemingly having played a major role in that serious car crash of late 1958—overwhelmed the mind of Morris Jessup in his final weeks and months.

Destabilizing Both Brain and Body

Such research may have been undertaken in the United Kingdom, too. When, in the mid-1980s, plans were formulated by the regime of then–Prime Minister Margaret Thatcher to base nuclear cruise missiles at strategic military bases in the British Isles, it provoked massive demonstrations on the part of Britain's general public—and particularly at a military establishment called Royal Air Force Greenham Common, in the county of Berkshire.

As a result of the planned placement of missiles at Greenham Common, a large group of female peace protesters set up camp outside the base. The protests were relatively peaceful—that is, until many of the women began to experience a series of disturbing symptoms, including deep depression, overwhelming anxiety attacks, intense migraine-like headaches, alarming losses of short-term memory, and much more of a distinctly mind-destabilizing nature. Theories began to quickly develop and circulate to the effect that the women were being specifically targeted with electromagnetic weaponry, as part of an intensive effort to bring their demonstrations—which had generated a large amount of support—to an abrupt and permanent end.

And this was no wide-eyed conspiracy theory, either: Even Britain's highly respected *Guardian* newspaper, which in 2013 broke the story of National Security Agency whistleblower Edward Snowden, reported the story in a serious fashion. In a March 10, 1986, article for the newspaper titled "Peace Women Fear Electronic Zapping at Base," journalist Gareth Parry reported: "The American military [at Greenham Common] have an intruder detection system called BISS, Base Installation Security System, which operates on a sufficiently high frequency to bounce radar waves off a human body moving in the vicinity of a perimeter fence" (Parry, 1986).

Altered States

So, what we have here is a formerly classified, official document of the Defense Intelligence Agency, ones that discusses a range of technologies that, as far back as the 1950s, were being secretly studied to determine how the human mind could be plunged into states of fear, stress, and depression, and how messages could be beamed into the head of a targeted person, to achieve a specific goal. One does not have to be a genius to note that the references to "military applications" of this very same technology suggest that making a murder look like a depression-driven suicide would not have been a difficult task in the slightest. And we have evidence of similar tactics utilized on citizens of the United Kingdom years later (Ibid.).

All of this data, and the documentation relative to the "Biological Effects of Electromagnetic Radiation (Radiowaves and Microwaves) Eurasian Communist Countries" report, is made more thought provoking by the fact that shortly after Charles Berlitz and William Moore's book, *The Philadelphia Experiment,* was published, Berlitz received in the mail a letter from a man in Arizona who appeared to know a great deal about the Adams and Williams report of 1976, including that "certain information was withheld from this report on national security grounds" (Genzlinger, 1981).

The man had much more to say, too, on the matter of radio-wave and microwave weapons: "The primary function of this system would be remote tracking and surveillance of a target person over a wide geographic area. An additional function of this apparatus could be remote monitoring of the sleep of the target person as to whether it is light, heavy or dreaming sleep, and the forcing of temporary physiological changes on the sleeping target person" (Ibid.).

On receipt of the letter, Berlitz forwarded it to Moore, who, in turn, provided a copy to Anna Lykins Genzlinger. Although Genzlinger got to speak with the man in question, and even learned his name, she chose not to pursue this avenue of research to its fullest degree for two reasons. Both of them were disturbing: Genzlinger felt the man's life might be put in danger if she did so; and after they discussed the source's revelations Moore advised Genzlinger, in no uncertain terms, that she "should not go any further with this for your own safety" (Ibid.).

Nevertheless, none of this prevented Genzlinger from telling those that read her book, as well as anyone else wanting to listen, that Jessup's death was far more than it seemed to be. Today, three decades after that renewed flurry of interest in the life and strange death of Morris Jessup, that is where matters continue to stand. Was it suicide? Could it have been murder? In a profoundly strange fashion, as we have now seen, it may very well have been a weird combination of both.

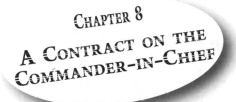

Wiping out the President

Shortly after he was elected president of the United States of America, Bill Clinton instructed his assistant attorney general, Webster Hubbell, to get to the bottom of two questions that he (Clinton) sorely wanted answering:

1. Who killed President John F. Kennedy at Dealey Plaza, in Dallas, Texas, on November 22, 1963?

2. Do UFOs really exist?

They were questions that, so far as we know, were not answered to the satisfaction of the president, if at all. As interested and intrigued as he was in such matters, even Clinton may not have been aware of a much bigger and wider issue—namely, the incredible possibility that both of those controversies to which he sought the answers were inextricably intertwined. That is to say, JFK was murdered by a ruthless and powerful cabal that was intent on preventing him from revealing to the world the truth about the UFO mystery. It might sound like the plot of a wild sci-fi movie of truly paranoid proportions. There are, however, strong indications that, far from being the stuff of fiction, it's actually the cold-blooded, astonishing truth. Let's take a look at the evidence.

On the matter of JFK's tragic and violent death on that fateful November 1963 afternoon, the official consensus—based upon the 1964 conclusions of the President's Commission on the Assassination of President Kennedy, which is far better known as the Warren Commission—is that the president was shot and killed by just one person. And we all know who that was: Lee Harvey Oswald. Not everyone was, or still is, in agreement, however. As evidence of this, in November 1998, a poll of U.S. citizens revealed that no less than 76 percent said they did not believe Oswald acted alone, and 77 percent were doubtful the truth of the matter would ever surface. Though many of those doubters might have been inclined to point fingers in the direction of the Cubans, the CIA, the Mafia, or the KGB, it's time to take the JFK assassination into realms of the otherworldly kind.

JFK and the Weird World of Flying Saucers

In 1988, while speaking about President Kennedy's secret knowledge of the "flying disk" mystery, UFO researcher John Lear said: "The powers that be had to eliminate President Kennedy because he wanted to release the information on the disks and the aliens in 1963. Since then, we have talked to people who have heard the recording made in the Oval Office when Kennedy pounded his fists [and said]: 'You guys better get your stuff together because I'm going to tell the public'" (Lear, 1987).

Lear, who took part in near-countless operations with the CIA and who holds each and every airman certificate ever issued by the Federal Aviation Administration, added: "There were several reasons why [John F. Kennedy] was assassinated. One was the Bay of Pigs fiasco; another was that he had threatened to 'shatter the CIA into a thousand pieces.' A third reason was because he threatened to pull all our Americans from Vietnam by 1965. The fourth was that he intended to expose the alien-disk cover up" (Ibid.). Lear is not alone in making such assertions.

In the early 1960s, William Holden, of the U.S. Air Force, was assigned to work on board the presidential plane, better known as Air Force One.

In the late 1990s, Holden went public with an account of what happened when, not long before the assassination, he (Holden) briefly engaged President Kennedy in a conversation about UFOs. It was a conversation that occurred on the plane itself and was prompted by Holden noticing JFK reading a newspaper article on the UFO controversy. His interest piqued, Holden took a deep breath and diplomatically asked the president what he thought about the subject. Holden got a surprising response. According to Holden, a very serious-looking Kennedy quietly replied that not only were UFOs real but it was his wish to reveal the truth to the public. There was, however, a problem: Kennedy continued that he was unable to share publicly what he knew on the subject for one very good reason: His hands were tied. By whom, we do not know.

Emmy Award–winning television producer and cattle-mutilation authority Linda Howe came across data suggesting that JFK was deeply frustrated by the profound level of secrecy that dominated the UFO issue. And, as investigative writer Lars Hansson noted after having met with Howe: "Ms. Howe described her meetings with military intelligence agents a few years before, during which the JFK assassination was discussed in some detail. After relating what they imparted to her she was most emphatic about the wisdom of leaving that issue alone" (Hansson, 1991).

Moving on, there is the matter of Colonel Philip Corso, co-author, with William Birnes, of the book *The Day After Roswell* that detailed his (Corso's) personal experiences working with extraterrestrial debris recovered outside of Roswell, New Mexico, in July 1947. Corso had another iron in the fire, however: Shortly before his 1998 death, Corso planned to reveal all he knew about the JFK assassination—which, apparently, was an enormous amount. The book, had it come to fruition, was to have been titled *The Day After Dallas*. Given Corso's UFO associations, one has to wonder if the book would have shed more light on the UFO-JFK connection.

Colonel Philip Corso had another tie to the killing of the president: He undertook investigative work for Richard Russell, who served as U.S. senator for Georgia from 1933 to 1971, and as chairman of the Senate Committee on Armed Services from 1955 to 1969. Russell was also a member of the Warren Commission that concluded JFK was murdered by Lee Harvey Oswald and by no one else. It transpires that back in the 1950s, Russell received a behind-closed-doors briefing on the issue of flying saucers from the CIA—the reason being that while on a fact-finding mission to the Soviet Union in 1955, Russell had a UFO sighting of close and significant proportions. It was a sighting that led to the creation of a U.S. Air Force Air Intelligence Information Report titled "Observations of Traveler in USSR," dated October 14, 1955.

Now we come to the matter of a controversial character that we crossed paths with earlier: Timothy Cooper.

A Secret Stash of UFO Files

As previously noted, a resident of Big Bear Lake, California, Timothy Cooper emerged quietly on the UFO scene in the early 1990s. By the mid-to-late '90s, however, Cooper was big news. Essentially, he claimed extensive contact with a variety of old-timers from the U.S. military and intelligence community who had provided him with mind-blowing data, and even official-looking documents, on crashed UFOs, recovered alien bodies, and even matters relative to the Kennedy assassination. Some researchers said the collective story of Cooper's sources—linked to a supposed highly secret group within officialdom known as Majestic 12 or MJ12—were just too good to be true. Others, however, were far less sure that nothing more than widespread fakery was at work.

As for the JFK-UFO issues contained in the Cooper collection, they were many and varied. In terms of their chronological order, the first document, titled "Interplanetary Phenomenon Unit Summary," dated from 1947 and made the controversial claim that Kennedy—a congressman at the time—knew of the notorious Roswell, New Mexico, crash that same year, almost immediately after it occurred. According to the unknown author of the document and in relation to the government's retrieval of an alien spacecraft outside of Roswell:

> It has become known to CIC [Counter-Intelligence Corps] that some of the recovery operation was shared with Representative John F. Kennedy, Massachusetts Democrat

elected to Congress in '46, son of Joseph P. Kennedy, Commission on Organization of the Executive Branch of the Government. Kennedy had limited duty as naval officer assigned to Naval Intelligence during the War. It is believed that information was obtained from source in Congress who is close to Secretary for Air Force (Wood and Wood, 1998).

Did JFK know of the truth of Roswell long before he became president? Just maybe, he did.

Moving on, there is a highly controversial, alleged CIA document that was provided to Cooper that maintains that the president shared some of his knowledge on the matters of crashed spacecraft and dead bodies of unknown origin with none other than his part-time lover, the legendary actress Marilyn Monroe. Possibly of relevance to this matter, the previously referenced Linda Howe has uncovered information—independent to that of Cooper—that relates to a visit to Area 51 (Nevada) by President Kennedy shortly after his election, allegedly to view the remains of recovered alien spacecraft.

It's also of note that the Monroe document references Dorothy Kilgallen, a noted journalist and friend to the actress. In 1955, and while vacationing in England, Kilgallen spoke with a senior figure in the British government who informed her that British authorities had recovered a severely wrecked UFO, as well as the remains of its crew, described as "small men." It was a story that Kilgallen splashed across the pages of the *Los Angeles Examiner* on May 23, 1955. She also had advance-access to certain portions of the Warren Commission report on JFK's death and was the last person to do a personal question-and-answer session with Jack Ruby, Lee Harvey Oswald's killer. A year after Kennedy's death, Kilgallen was telling just about anyone and everyone who would listen that she was going to cause major controversy by revealing something new and astonishing that concerned the president's murder in Dealey Plaza. She did nothing of the sort, however. What Kilgallen *did* do, however, in 1965, was to die. Whatever the journalist knew, she took it to the grave (Kilgallen, 1955).

Was JFK assassinated at Dealey Plaza in Dallas, Texas, because of UFOs? (Nick Redfern, 2001)

And as researchers William Jones and Rebecca Minshall noted: "On November 8, 1965, fifty-two-year-old Ms. Kilgallen died in her home of acute ethanol and barbiturate intoxication, the circumstances of which were undetermined. A close friend and confidante reportedly died of undetermined causes two days later" (Jones and Minshall, 1991).

A purportedly highly classified paper provided to Cooper, dated June 28, 1961, and from JFK to Allen Dulles, then-director of the Central Intelligence Agency, urgently requested a "review of MJ12 Intelligence Operations as they relate to Cold War Psychological Warfare Plans" (Wood and Wood, 1998). If the document is genuine, then JFK, even as far back as 1961, was gunning for the alien answers.

The papers state that Dulles, who was ousted from his position as director of the CIA in September 1961, said that MJ12's major concern at the time was not the UFO issue itself, per se. Rather, there was a deep-seated fear that the Soviets might misinterpret a fleet of real UFOs for incoming American nuclear warheads, and, as a result, a catastrophic Third World War would erupt. Dulles, the Cooper files state, told the president in concerned fashion: "The overall effectiveness about the actual Soviet response and alert status is not documented to the point where U.S. intelligence can provide a true picture of how Soviet air defense perceive unidentified flying objects" (Ibid.).

Realizing that a worldwide nuclear war might be provoked not by human aggression but by a mistakenly identified armada of alien craft, the Cooper files say JFK felt that he had no choice but to secretly share with the Russians the U.S. government's most guarded UFO information—not because the president had a particular desire to do so, but because he felt it was the only way to prevent the end of civilization resulting from a catastrophic blunder. The result, according to yet another of the Cooper papers, was that soon thereafter JFK ordered NASA's director, James Webb, to develop a program with the Soviet Union in joint space and lunar exploration, and stressed the need to help the Soviets understand the differences between genuine UFOs and high-flying military hardware of the U.S. military.

Kennedy, Khrushchev, and the UFO Problem

Of all the Cooper files that reference JFK and UFOs, without doubt the most controversial (and, some might say, wholly outrageous) is that which is alleged to be a transcript of a 1963 telephone conversation between Kennedy and the Soviet premier, Nikita Khrushchev. With the title of "UFO Working Groups," it reads like this:

> Kennedy: "Mr. Premiere, a situation has developed that affects both our countries and the world and I feel it necessary to convey to you a problem that we share in common."

> Khrushchev: "Mr. President, I agree."

> Kennedy: "As you must appreciate the tension between our two great nations has often brought us to the brink of showmanship with all the tapestry of a Greek comedy and our impasse last year [Author's note: This is almost certainly a reference to the

Cuban Missile Crisis of 1962] was foolish and deadly. The division that separates us is through misunderstanding, politics, and cultural differences. But we have one thing in common which I would like to address to your working group on the UFO problem."

Khrushchev: "Yes, yes, I agree with your assessment. We nearly tied the knot that divides us permanently. Our working group believes the same way as yours. The UFO problem presents grave dangers."

Kennedy: "Then you agree, Mr. Premiere, that we should cooperate together on this issue?"

Khrushchev: "Yes, Mr. President."

Kennedy: "Mr. Premiere, I have begun an initiative with our NASA to exchange information with your Academy of Sciences in which I hope will foster mutual concern over this problem and hopefully find some resolution. I have also instructed our CIA to provide me with full disclosure on the phantom aspects and classified programs in which I can better assess the situation. Can you persuade your KGB to do likewise?"

Khrushchev: "Mr. President, I cannot guarantee full cooperation in this area but I owe it to future history and the security of our planet to try. As you must know I have been somewhat limited in my official capacity as Party Chairman to order such cooperation in this area. We too feel that the UFO is a matter of highest importance to our collective security. If I can arrange for a secret meeting between our working groups at a secret location and at a time designated by you, I feel that this much on my part can happen."

Kennedy: "Mr. Premiere, if a meeting at this level can convene it will be an important first step. It will lead to more dialog and trust between our countries and reduce the ever present threat of nuclear war."

Khrushchev: "Yes, Mr. President, it will."

Kennedy: "Then we are in agreement."

Khrushchev: "Yes."

Kennedy: "Yes. Until we talk again" (Wood and Wood, 1998).

In the scenario outlined to Timothy Cooper, Majestic 12 was wholly against sharing with the Soviets all that it knew about the flying saucer phenomenon, even if doing so might have reduced the risk of an accidental nuclear war. Coupled with the president's determination to bring down the U.S. government's house of UFO secrets, the members of Majestic 12 saw only one option in their future: Kennedy had to go, as in permanently. It would not be long before Dealey Plaza, in Dallas, Texas, was chosen as the place where JFK would take his last breaths, something that was guaranteed to ensure the government's policy of overwhelming UFO secrecy remained intact. Such a scenario is bolstered by yet another batch of MJ12-originated documentation that expresses concerns about inquiries Kennedy had made "regarding our activities which we cannot allow" and "sensitive files that would connect MJ12 to JFK's murder" (Ibid.).

Bill Cooper: From JFK to UFOs to RIP

Forget Lee Harvey Oswald. JFK was killed by the man behind the wheel, in full view of the people of Dallas and thousands of cameras. That was the outrageous claim of one of the most vocal conspiracy theorists of the 1980s and 1990s. His name was Milton William "Bill" Cooper. The man who Cooper fingered as the guilty party was William Greer, a Secret Service agent who drove the presidential limousine on the day that JFK was destined not to leave Dallas alive. When shots echoed around Dealey Plaza, Greer slowed the car down and turned back to look at the president.

For Cooper, Greer's actions were not due to confusion caused by the chaos breaking out all around him. No. Cooper claimed that analysis of the famous footage taken by Abraham Zapruder, on the grassy knoll on November 22, showed Greer pointing some form of device at JFK. That device, Cooper maintained to anyone that would listen, was nothing less than a sci-fi-style weapon developed by government personnel that had acquired the technology from extraterrestrials. Needless to say, very few had any time at all for *that* claim!

By the time Cooper got on his rant, which began in the late 1980s, Greer wasn't around to defend himself. He passed away in 1985 from cancer, having retired from the Secret Service in 1966 as a result of problems caused by a stomach ulcer. In a strange piece of irony, Cooper himself died by the bullet. In the summer of 1998, he was formerly charged with tax evasion. Cooper told the government where to go and what to do. What the government did, on November 5, 2001, was to dispatch deputies to Cooper's Arizona home. A shootout soon erupted. Cooper, like JFK, was soon full of lead.

This, in essence, all amounts to the *unofficial* story of the JFK-UFO connection. To be sure, it's quite a saga, to say the very least. But can it be vindicated? Is there any evidence to suggest that JFK actually was gunned down to prevent the world knowing the truth about UFOs? Incredibly, such a scenario cannot be ruled out.

Kennedy, NASA, and the Race for Space

There's no doubt at all that in the lead-up to his death on November 22, 1963, JFK *was* taking a proactive stance on the matter of outer space affairs. As a perfect example, on September 12, 1962, JFK gave a very well-received lecture at Rice Stadium (Houston, Texas), in which he explained his plans for America's role in the world of off-Earth travel:

> The exploration of space will go ahead, whether we join in
> it or not, and it is one of the great adventures of all time,
> and no nation which expects to be the leader of other
> nations can expect to stay behind in the race for space....

> We set sail on this new sea because there is new knowledge
> to be gained, and new rights to be won, and they must be
> won and used for the progress of all people.... We choose
> to go to the Moon. We choose to go to the Moon in this
> decade and do the other things, not because they are easy,
> but because they are hard, because that goal will serve to
> organize and measure the best of our energies and skills,
> because that challenge is one that we are willing to accept,
> one we are unwilling to postpone, and one which we intend
> to win (NASA, 2013).

Moving on, only 10 days before he was assassinated, Kennedy sent controversial instructions to NASA director James Webb. Under cover of National Security Action Memorandum No. 271, the president told Webb to "assume personally the initiative and central responsibility within the government for the development of a program of substantive cooperation with the Soviet Union in the field of outer space, including the development of specific technical proposals" (National Security Act Memorandum No. 271..., 2013). More amazing, Kennedy even told Webb that such cooperation should extend to "lunar landing programs" (Ibid.). That this document is 100 percent legitimate is not in doubt: It surfaced via the terms of the Freedom of Information Act.

Briefings at Brooks AFB

On November 21, 1963, just one day before JFK's death in the city of Dallas, a highly significant event occurred at Brooks Air Force Base in Texas: President Kennedy opened half a dozen new buildings dedicated to aerospace medical research, such as how to protect American astronauts in outer space from the effects of zero gravity and radiation. It was JFK's very last official task as president. While at Brooks, Kennedy met with two notable individuals. One was Major General Theodore C. Bedwell, Jr., who, from 1946 to 1947, was deputy surgeon and chief, industrial medicine, Air Materiel Command at Wright Field, Ohio—the name of which was changed, in 1948, when Wright Field and Patterson Field became Wright-Patterson Air Force Base.

Wright Field just happened to be the location to which numerous military old-timers have claimed alien bodies recovered near Roswell, New Mexico, in early July 1947 were secretly taken for autopsy. Kennedy also received a briefing at Brooks from Colonel Harold V. Ellingson, USAF, previously the post surgeon and hospital commander at Fort Detrick, Maryland. Perhaps not entirely coincidental: For years rumors have circulated to the effect that highly classified research into alien bodies, and even deadly extraterrestrial viruses, has been carried out at Fort Detrick.

From Maury Island to JFK

It must be said that more than a few UFO researchers have suggested the Maury Island affair of June 1947 (and the subject of Chapter 1 of this book) was nothing but a hoax, one perpetrated by Fred Crisman, with Harold Dahl playing a subservient role, that got tragically and disastrously out of hand when First Lieutenant Frank Mercer Brown and Captain William Lee Davidson were killed. On the other hand, however, it's an undeniable fact that Crisman had a most intriguing post–Maury Island life, one that placed him right in the middle of the Kennedy assassination.

From 1961 to 1973, Jim Garrison was the district attorney of New Orleans, Louisiana, and the man whose book, *On the Trail of the Assassins,* was a major inspiration for Oliver Stone's 1991 movie, *JFK,* which told of Garrison's efforts to try to figure out the truth behind JFK's death. Although UFOs do not feature in *JFK,* or in Garrison's book, Garrison identified key players in the murder of Kennedy who most assuredly *did* have deep-running UFO connections.

During the course of Garrison's investigations, the name of none other than Fred Crisman came up on more than a few occasions—specifically as someone allegedly linked to the killing of JFK, and maybe even *directly* involved. Rather amazingly, Garrison finally came to believe that Crisman was actually none other than the legendary second gunman in the assassination, positioned behind the equally legendary grassy knoll at the time of the nation-changing event. Although the case against Crisman was not strong enough to bring to court or confirm anything definitive, it's intriguing that William Torbitt, the pseudonymous source behind a 1970 book, *Nomenclature of an Assassination Cabal*, made no bones at all about fingering Crisman as one of three hoboes taken into custody right after the killing of the president and who *were* found hanging around in the rail yard that sat next to Dealey Plaza's grassy knoll.

On a similar path, one of Garrison's key targets of investigation was a man named Clay Shaw, who Garrison believed was a leading player in the conspiracy to murder JFK. Although the mainstream media scoffed at Garrison's claims of conspiracy, in 1977 official documents surfaced showing that Shaw—who played a leading role in the creation of the New Orleans–based International Trade Mart—had been an asset of the CIA's Domestic Contact Service since at least 1949. More astonishing, a confidante of Garrison informed him that Fred Crisman was the first person Shaw telephoned after being informed he was in major trouble. Interestingly, Crisman also held the position of bishop with the Universal Life Church (ULC), an organization created in 1962 by the Reverend Kirby James Hensley, a man who once ran for president but who, rather oddly, never learned to read or write. Possibly of relevance: The ULC was infiltrated by the CIA in the 1960s, an operation in which Crisman may have played a significant role.

The Banister Connection

Guy Banister was one of the first FBI agents that investigated UFO events for J. Edgar Hoover, when Hoover instructed his personnel, in the summer of 1947, to assist the Army Air Force in its UFO inquiries and studies. The most notorious UFO case that Banister investigated occurred in Twin Falls, Idaho, in July 1947. It's one that ties Banister directly to the crashed UFO controversy. The following is extracted from the *Tacoma News Tribune* of July 12, 1947 (Tacoma, of course, being the location of the notorious Maury Island affair):

> FBI agent W.G. Banister said an object which appeared to be a "flying disk" was found early today at Twin Falls, Ida., and turned over to federal authorities there. Banister, Special Agent in Charge of the FBI in Montana and Idaho, said the bureau had reported the discovery to the army at

Fort Douglas, Utah. An FBI agent in Twin Falls inspected the "saucer" and described it as similar to the "cymbals used by a drummer in a band, placed face to face." The object measured 30 ½ inches in diameter, with a metal dome about 14 inches high on the opposite side, anchored in place by what appeared to be stove bolts. The gadget is gold plated on one side and silver (either stainless-steel, aluminum or tin) on the other. It appeared to have been turned out by machine, reports from Twin Falls said. The FBI declined to elaborate further ("FBI Drums Up...", 1947).

This particular incident was ultimately proved to have been nothing more than a good-natured prank, though initially it caused waves of alarm amongst the FBI and the Army, something that led Banister to be briefed on salient points of the UFO issue by military personnel from Fort Douglas, Utah. Even today, decades later, we still don't know exactly what Banister was told about the wave of flying saucer sightings in the summer of 1947. What we do know, however, is that 16 years later Banister became forever linked to the shooting of JFK.

At the time of the Kennedy assassination, Guy Banister was retired from the FBI and had his own detective agency in New Orleans: Guy Banister Associates. He soon came to the attention of Jim Garrison, partly because of a Banister-Oswald connection: The building in which Banister's office was housed had two addresses, one of which was used by Oswald when he was doing work for the Fair Play for Cuba Committee. Banister was also linked to David Ferrie, a skilled pilot tied to the CIA-funded Cuban Democratic Revolutionary Front.

Interestingly, Jim Garrison knew Banister back in the 1940s, as his own words reveal: "When he was in the police department, we had lunch together now and then, swapping colorful stories about our earlier careers in the FBI. A ruddy-faced man with blue eyes which stared right at you, he dressed immaculately and always wore a small rosebud in his lapel" (Ibid.).

That, at the time, Garrison and Banister were in Tacoma, makes it more than possible that both men knew of the Maury Island events, too.

Lee Harvey Oswald and Area 51

There's even a Lee Harvey Oswald connection to all this. It transpires that David Ferrie and Lee Harvey Oswald served together in the same Civil Air Patrol unit in the 1950s, specifically the New Orleans Cadet Squadron, based at Lakefront Airport, which Oswald joined in July 1955. And here's where it gets even more interesting: In October 1962, Oswald went to work for a Texas-based company called Jaggars-Chiles-Stovall. It was a company that undertook classified photo-analysis connected to the CIA's U-2 spy-plane program. Where was the U-2 developed? Area 51, that's where. And we all know what goes on out there, right?

It's also worth noting that in 1979, the House Select Committee on Assassinations (HSCA), which looked into the matter of Kennedy's death and concluded there *was* a conspiracy to kill the president, recorded in its report that HSCA members had uncovered strong evidence of a link (albeit an unclear link) among Oswald, Ferrie, and Shaw that could be traced back to about 12 weeks before JFK was shot.

Is it possible that Oswald, Ferrie, Shaw, Banister, and Crisman were all hired by a shadowy cabal that wanted JFK dead because of his plans to go public with what he knew about the UFO phenomenon? It may sound incredible, yet, as we have seen, undeniable UFO threads run right through pretty much the entirety of the Kennedy assassination saga. And hiring people who may have been in on the UFO secrets from the very beginning in 1947—specifically Banister and Crisman—and who understood the need to maintain the saucer-filled status quo, makes even greater sense.

More than 50 years after President Kennedy's tragic death shocked not just a nation but the entire world, the events of November 22, 1963 are still shrouded in mystery and intrigue—much to the satisfaction of certain, powerful figures in officialdom that know the truth about UFOs, one strongly suspects.

CHAPTER 9
THE MICROWAVE INCIDENT

We Have Contact

Scoriton (which can also be spelled Scorriton) is a small, old village located in the English county of Devonshire. It is surrounded by wild but picturesque countryside and even has its very own resident ancient stone circle, one that was built during prehistoric times. Scoriton borders upon the sprawling Dartmoor National Park, where Sir Arthur Conan Doyle set his classic Sherlock Holmes novel *The Hound of the Baskervilles.* It is, without doubt, a village filled with old-world atmosphere, and echoes of times and people long gone. But there is something else about Scoriton: It may well have been the site of a profound UFO encounter that ended in controversial and mysterious death. Although the event in question occurred on April 24, 1965, we first have to address what happened exactly one day earlier, when one of the most lauded, laughed at, criticized, and revered characters in Ufology died: George Adamski, a man with more than a few links to our old friend Karl Hunrath, who mysteriously vanished in 1953.

Polish by birth, Adamski was, without doubt, the most famous (and infamous) of all the so-called "Contactees." From the early 1950s onward, numerous people, particularly on the West Coast of the United States, claimed contact with eerily human-looking aliens that became known as the Space Brothers. Supposedly benevolent, but not without a few bullying, self-important, and fascist-style tendencies, they got chummy with the likes of Adamski, as a means to warn the world of the overwhelming perils posed by atomic weapons. Adamski's claims of alien contact were as wild as they were fascinating. They also caught the imagination of the public, as is evidenced by the fact that his 1953 book *Flying Saucers Have Landed,* co-written with Desmond Leslie, became a huge hit. Not even the Space Brothers could save Adamski from the clutches of the reaper, however: He died of a heart attack, in Maryland, on April 23, 1965, at the age of 74. Only one day later, however, matters of the Adamski kind were unfolding in sleepy old Scoriton.

Invited Onto a UFO

Edward Bryant was a man with a notably varied background. In his 20s, he worked as a seaman and, during the Second World War, served with the British Commandos, an elite arm of the military that succeeded in inflicting major damage on the Nazi war-machine. In the immediate post-war period, Bryant moved to the island of Gibraltar, where he was employed in the field of security, and, in the 1950s, returned to his native England, specifically to Scoriton. By 1965, however, Bryant, then age 51, had opted for a quieter life: He was paid to tend the grounds of a nursing home in Newton-Abbott, a Devonshire town, the origins of which date back to Neolithic times, located about 13 miles from Scoriton.

According to Bryant—who ultimately shared his story with a UFO researcher named Eileen Buckle and which was also investigated by Norman Oliver, of the British UFO Research Association BUFORA—on the day in question he was working in the yard of his home when he saw something amazing. It was nothing less than a definitive flying saucer hovering, at very low level, over a field near his home. Amazed and shocked, Bryant approached the edge of the field in decidedly tentative fashion, but was reportedly motioned to come closer by what he described as a trio of humanoid beings, dressed in headgear and silver outfits somewhat akin to those worn by deep-sea divers, and standing around the significantly sized saucer. Although by now deathly afraid, Bryant took a deep breath and slowly moved closer.

As he got up close and personal, so to speak, Bryant could see that the strange entities displayed subtle differences to the average person: They seemed to have difficulty breathing in our atmosphere, they lacked thumbs, and their foreheads were noticeably elongated, which became apparent when they removed their helmets. Those issues aside, the three—one of whom, oddly, looked to be only in his early to mid-teens—appeared to be pretty much normal. In a vaguely American accent, the youngest of the three introduced himself to Bryant as "Yamski," and claimed that he and his kind originated on the planet Venus, the supposed point of origin of many of George Adamski's alien buddies. Apparently realizing that Bryant was looking on not unlike the proverbial deer caught in the proverbial headlights, the alien remarked to his colleagues that "[i]f only Des [Author's note: or possibly "Les," Bryant told Buckle] were here, he would understand" (Bowen, 1969).

At that point, something incredible, and not a little daunting, occurred: Bryant was invited aboard the UFO to take a tour. The craft, as far as Bryant could tell, was split into three segments, none of which displayed anything in the way of technology or propulsion systems. Certainly, all that could be seen in each room were a couch and something that vaguely resembled a television set. One of the aliens then added: "Watch out for the blue light in the evenings; in a month's time we will bring you proof of Mantell," clearly a reference to the ill-fated Captain Thomas Mantell, whose 1948 death has previously been addressed in this book (Ibid.). With that, Bryant was motioned to leave the spacecraft and watched, from a distance of about 30 feet, as the aliens waved goodbye and their craft vanished—as in literally vanished (Ibid.).

Unwelcome Publicity and an Investigation

Sure enough, the aliens kept their word: Late one night, about six weeks later, what was assumed by Bryant to be the very same UFO flew low over the cottage in which he and his family lived, making a loud, echoing noise as it did so. On the morning after, just as dawn was breaking, Bryant left his home for work in nearby Newton Abbott, but was delayed by the discovery of two things on the ground: a strange, glowing piece of metal and a small container, in which was a piece of parchment. It was a parchment that read *Adelphos Adelpho*.

Unsure what to do, Bryant, after a few days spent quietly pondering on the matter, confided in his wife, who, in no uncertain terms, told him he was talking complete and utter nonsense. Unknown to the Bryants, their children overheard the conversation and, as a result, it wasn't long before all the local schoolchildren, the people of Scoriton, and even the police knew about Bryant's strange claims. Nor did it take long before the rumor mill churned wildly and suggested that, rather than aliens having landed in sleepy old Scoriton, the event had been provoked by the emergency landing of nothing less than a Soviet spacecraft!

Faced with the fact that just about everyone and his brother in the area knew of his tale of the extraterrestrial kind, Bryant chose to pen a letter to the local newspaper to try to lay matters to rest by telling the story as *he* recalled it—rather than as everyone around Scoriton was telling it. It was as a result of going public that Bryant caught the attention of the aforementioned Eileen Buckle and Norman Oliver. The combined research of both investigators yielded yet further details. Interestingly, a careful check of Bryant's home revealed nothing to suggest he had any previous interest in UFOs. The family's bookshelves displayed not even a single title on the subject, and Bryant seemed to be genuinely mystified by the entire saga.

Not only that, both Buckle and Oliver could not fail to notice that the name of one of the aliens was "Yamski," which was very similar to Adamksi. Moreover, the references to "Des" and/or "Les" was suggestive of Adamski's co-author on *Flying Saucers Have Landed*, Desmond Leslie. That Adamski died only one day before Bryant's encounter only muddled matters even more. Then there was the matter of the strange piece of metal that Bryant found outside of his home. Incredibly, it *was* found to have come from an aircraft, but it was never shown to have been, as the aliens supposedly claimed to Bryant, "proof of Mantell" (Ibid.).

Eileen Buckle, who wrote an entire book on the case—*The Scoriton Mystery*—remained open minded on the whole affair and gave Bryant the benefit of the doubt. Norman Oliver, however, was far less open minded and concluded that the entire matter was a hoax dreamed up by Bryant. Unfortunately, it was impossible to ascertain the facts completely, as Bryant, on June 24, 1967—and when the investigation was still very much going on—died suddenly from the effects of a fast-acting brain tumor.

And it's now that we come to the most disturbing aspect of the Scoriton saucer and Edward Bryant. And why is it so disturbing? Simple: It suggests that Bryant's death by brain-tumor was provoked by his UFO encounter, albeit in a decidedly alternative and incredible fashion.

Blowing the Whistle

At one point or another, most UFO researchers will cross paths with what might be termed a Ufological whistleblower, one who wishes to impart highly classified data on UFOs, as a means to help get the truth out to the research community, the public, and the media. For Rich Reynolds, a much-respected investigator of the UFO puzzle, such a conspiratorial crossing of paths occurred in the late 1970s. It was back then that Reynolds was contacted by a decidedly Machiavellian character named Bosco Nedelcovic—a man whose first name, rather oddly, was the same as that of Karl Hunrath's aircraft-destroying machine that caused both the FBI and George Adamski so much grief in 1953. Now dead, Nedelcovic was a Yugoslavian employed, in the 1950s, by the U.S. Department of State's Agency for International Development (AID), which also had deep and winding links to the CIA. In later years, Nedelcovic worked on highly classified programs for the Department of Defense. He was, as one might astutely assume, a man with many fingers in just about as many secret pies.

According to Nedelcovic, in the 1960s, secret elements of officialdom were engaged in the deliberate fabrication of UFO events using controversial methods similar to those that were born out of the CIA's MKULTRA project that began in the 1950s—and that, as we have seen, led to the 1953 death of U.S. Army biochemist Frank Olson. That's to say, mind-altering cocktails, coupled with hallucinogenic drugs, were being used on unwitting members of the general public to convince them they had undergone encounters of the extraterrestrial variety when the reality was very different. As for the reasons behind this strange project, they appear to have been distinctly twofold:

1. To determine how successfully the human brain could be scrambled into thinking it had experienced something incredible that actually had no reality to it, and

2. To stage-manage faked, mind-manipulated events to try to figure out how the general populace might react to *real* encounters with extraterrestrials, should such entities one day appear en masse.

Reynolds listened carefully as Nedelcovic told his controversial but undeniably captivating story. In 1963 Nedelcovic transferred from AID to the Department of Defense (DoD). Because Nedelcovic was fluent in more than a few languages, and his job with the DoD was in the field of translation, he spent a great deal of time traveling overseas, particularly to Europe. Much of Nedelcovic's overseas work was focused upon preparing briefings for personnel from the CIA, NATO, the U.S. Air Force, and the U.S. Navy.

Between 1964 and 1965, said Nedelcovic, plans were initiated to fabricate certain "UFO episodes" in both England and the United States (Reynolds, 2006). They were to be highly sophisticated operations involving not just mind-altering technology but "visual displays, radar displacement, and artifact droppings" (Ibid.). In the UK, they were reportedly coordinated out of a British Royal Air Force base called Lakenheath, located in Suffolk, England. One of the U.S.-based events of the fabricated variety was said to have occurred at Exeter, New Hampshire, about five months after the events at Scoriton. Such was the controversy surrounding the matter, a book was written on the case in 1966. Its title, very appropriately, was *Incident at Exeter.* The book told of how, one night in September 1965, a man named Norman Muscarello had a very close encounter with something assumed to be unearthly in the skies near Exeter. The author was none other than John G. Fuller, hardly a stranger to the world of MKULTRA, mind control, and the death of Frank Olson, as was demonstrated in a previous chapter (Ibid.).

As Rich Reynolds noted, Nedelcovic explained to him that at a CIA briefing in January 1969, he (Nedelcovic) was told of an unfortunate and fatal episode. Although Nedelcovic did not know the name of the individual whose life came to an end after being plunged into a world filled with faked, mind-bending UFOs, the briefing referenced Eileen Buckle's book, making it clear to Reynolds that Nedelcovic was clearly referring to Edward Bryant (Ibid.).

The Scoriton Affair Becomes Deadly

Bosco Nedelcovic continued that after Edward Bryant contacted BUFORA with the details of his extraordinary encounter, CIA officials quietly visited Bryant and "decided to subject the witness to further UFO experience." Reynolds recalls:

> The man [Bryant] was taken to London where he accepted the offer to have his story verified by the use of a "truth seeking drug." During this session a doctor administered experimental drugs used to induce specific hallucinatory material into a subject's brain processes. In this case the man was also stimulated by microwave transmissions so that material induced would be retained upon awakening as if real events. [Nedelcovic] said he saw reports of many such episodes but this was the only one he remembers as having a death attributed directly to the experiment itself (Ibid.).

The death of Bryant—from "excessive experimentation," Nedelcovic informed Reynolds—was provoked by "the injudicious use of microwave technology" (Ibid.). It was so injudicious that it apparently led elements of both the CIA and the National Security Agency to be admonished over what became known, within officialdom, as "the microwave incident" (Ibid.).

PROPOSAL FOR THE ESTABLISHMENT OF A

"SOCIAL SUSTENANCE PROGRAM"

IN A SITUATION OF EXTREME POVERTY AND UNDERDEVELOPMENT

Discussion Draft - July 1975

by Bosco Nedelcovic
6001 North 18th St.
Arlington, Virginia 22205

Introduction

The scenario I am about to sketch pertains to a small island-state or island-province, somewhere in the Caribbean. It has little usable land and considerable population density. It has few basic industries - probably sugar and rhum, some agriculture and dairy production, some construction activity, maybe an oil refinery or some other extractive industry, and of course tourism. But all these combined cannot begin to provide enough employment for the native population. In fact, unemployment is already high and getting worse - if nothing else, due to sheer population growth and an expanding labor force - and emigration to the mainland has virtually come to a halt.

Family planning is getting attention but its results will take years. Meanwhile the situation is becoming increasingly grim for large segments of the population. Pockets of subsistence agriculture are fast disappearing, and caring for unemployed family members or relatives is straining personal ties to the breaking point. Direct government assistance to the poor - other than some housing and health services - is minimal or nonexistent in view of budgetary limitations. Social inequities are becoming more apparent and harder to bear, and growing frustration, social unrest and criminality are understandably on the rise.

On top of that, international developments look ominous. Tourism, which has provided a substantial share of the island's income up to now, may suffer a severe drop as a result of the recession affecting the mainland. At the same time the island is compelled to pay higher prices for everything it imports - particularly oil and food. The local tax base shrinks precisely when the need for government services is greatest. Foreign aid and other forms of international assistance are about to dry up; even private charities and foundations are hard pressed to keep up with needed social programs. And as foreign investments and overseas markets become harder to tap, the island is in a desperate crunch to survive both financially and socially.

Correspondence between Bosco Nedelcovic and the CIA (CIA, 1975).

In essence, that is the story of Bosco Nedelcovic. To be sure, it's a highly controversial one. Nevertheless, as we have seen in the matter of the mysterious death of Frank Olson, the CIA's MKULTRA program of the 1950s was most certainly not without its fatalities. That a further fatality, one borne out of microwave exposure, may have occurred in the 1960s is not at all implausible. There is something else worth commenting on: Eileen Buckle and Norman Oliver were not the only ones that dug deep into the cosmic claims of Edward Bryant.

Robert Chapman, the science correspondent for the UK's *Sunday Express* newspaper, also got on the case and published his findings in 1969. It's entirely possible that Chapman may have heard rumors or snippets of "the microwave incident" story, because he curiously wrote, when summing up his feelings on Bryant's claims: "There remains a possibility, of course, that [Bryant] *might* have had the UFO sighting planted in his mind through hypnotism" (Chapman, 1981). Chapman also, rather intriguingly, addressed the possibility that the UFO landing as reported by Bryant had been "staged" (Ibid.). Although Chapman finally dismissed all talk of a staged event and attendant hypnotism, it's decidedly notable that he even brought those two issues up *at all*—given that such comments dovetail very nicely with the assertions of Bosco Nedelcovic.

If Bryant's 1967 death—at the age of just 53—*was* due to the reckless use of microwave technology and "drugs used to induce specific hallucinatory material into a subject's brain processes" (Reynolds, 2006), then, at the *very* least, the guilty parties should be made to stand trial for manslaughter, if they are still with us. If, however, they, too, have since gone to the grave, then the Scoriton mystery will very likely remain the enigma that it was all those decades ago. There is just one thing we can be sure of in this twist-filled tale: Only two years after undergoing a strange UFO encounter in the pleasant English countryside, the previously healthy Edward Bryant was stone dead.

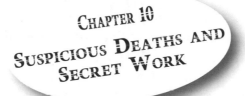

CHAPTER 10
SUSPICIOUS DEATHS AND
SECRET WORK

Fatalities in the Defense World

In the early to mid-1970s, a number of individuals working for a leading defense contractor in the United Kingdom died under highly suspicious and dubious circumstances. Rather notably, they were all employed by, or undertook contract-based work for, a company called Marconi Electronic Systems. Also known as GEC-Marconi, it was, in 1999, taken over by British Aerospace and is now known as BAE Systems Electronics Limited. It's a company whose research is at the forefront of cutting-edge technologies in the fields of advanced weaponry, electronics, lasers, underwater-based weapon systems, and space-satellite components. More intriguing is the fact that the location where the unfortunate souls worked became a brief hotspot for UFO activity.

The first death in question, which occurred in 1973, involved a man named Robert Wilson, a former employee of a Marconi factory in the English town of Chelmsford. The story came to light when a British newspaper, the *Sunday Telegraph,* splashed the details across its pages. And a decidedly strange story it was, too. Wilson was employed by Marconi until 1971, after which time he would have had nothing else to do with the company had it not been for one thing: While cleaning out the loft of his home one day in 1972, Wilson found a pile of "confidential Marconi documents" that originated with his former employer (Evans and Bartholomew, 2009). Precisely how they got there was never made clear. Concerned over security issues, Wilson quickly visited the Marconi facility and explained the situation. After an intense grilling by senior personnel, and having handed the top-secret documents over, Wilson returned home. Then something very strange happened: The next day, Wilson accidentally shot himself in the chest with a pistol he was in the middle of cleaning—while it was *loaded*. Fortunately he survived.

Wilson told a reporter from the *Sunday Telegraph*: "The nature of the blunder lay in the fact that I was handling the pistol while the muzzle was pointing towards me. It was an error so grotesque that I have shivers" (Collins, 1990). It's ironic that the article in question was titled "Mystery of the Shot Marconi Expert," because the mystery had barely begun. One year later, Wilson was dead. He was found in his garage, overcome by carbon-monoxide fumes, not unlike Morris K. Jessup in a certain Florida park 14 years previously. Very oddly, it seemed that Wilson had been working on his car with the engine running and the garage door shut. And then there came another development.

Practically no time at all after Robert Wilson's death, a young man named Gerard Jack Darlow died in his small, Chelmsford apartment, from a deep knife wound to the chest. Twenty-two-year-old Darlow, too, worked in the very same Marconi facility as had Wilson. The official verdict was that the fatal wound that ended Darlow's life in May 1973 was self-inflicted.

Marconi's UFOs

Rather notably, during the same time frame that Gerard Jack Darlow died, there was a series of UFO sightings over the Marconi complex at which both he and Robert Wilson worked. Prepared by an arm of the British Police Force called Special Branch—one of the key roles of which is to investigate terrorism-based activity in the UK—is a now-declassified document on the encounters titled "Unidentified Aircraft—Marconi, New Street, Chelmsford, May 12, 1973." The file in question chiefly focuses on the possibility that the unidentified aircraft may have been a helicopter flown by the Irish Republican Army (IRA), which was indeed a major threat to the UK at the time, though it also contains a few UFO-themed overtones.

8A

WEST YORKSHIRE

METROPOLITAN POLICE

P.O. Box 9, Wakefield, WF1 3QP

Telephone: Wakefield 75222, ext. 300

Our reference: GAO/GK

Your reference: 371/74/94

8 August 1974

CONFIDENTIAL

Dear Sir

With reference to your letter of the 1 August 1974, the replies received to date from other Forces, to the request for a check to be made on all known helicopters and helicopter pilots, already have disclosed useful items of intelligence. The full extent of this intelligence cannot be assessed, of course, until all Forces have reported the results of their enquiries but so far there are indications that many follow-up enquiries will have to be made into the background of "dubious" helicopter operators and pilots. There is, however, every indication that the exercise will prove worthwhile and all the information when collated and indexed will be available to all Forces in the United Kingdom.

It is felt that the threat of the use of helicopters in subversive or extremist activities cannot be ignored and, if the exercise is to be successful, then it is essential that checks be made on all existing helicopters and known pilots in this country, whether registered or unregistered.

It is appreciated that so far as you are concerned the enquiries which will have to be made to seek the information we have requested will prove to be a drain on your available manpower and, as a result, will be somewhat protracted. Regardless of this, and particularly in view of the existing terrorist threat, it will be appreciated if you can arrange for appropriate action to be taken, as outlined in my letter of the 18 July 1974.

Yours faithfully

Assistant Chief Constable (Crime)

An extract from the British Police Force's files on UFOs and other mysterious helicopters in the 1970s (Special Branch, 1974).

For example, the craft—which appeared three times in the early hours of May 12, 1973—was described as being silent, illuminated by a solitary bright blue light, and lost from view by ascending vertically, turning off its light, and vanishing from sight. Rather notably, the file includes the transcript of an interview with a security guard patrolling the facility at the time, one whose name is excised from the released records. Or, rather, it's *meant* to be excised.

Those within officialdom that carefully blacked out certain sections of the Special Branch papers prior to their declassification overlooked one mention of the man's last name, which is revealed as "Mr. Dalloway." Utterly baffling, but also deeply interesting, given the deaths of both Robert Wilson and Gerard Jack Darlow, Dalloway told the interviewing Special Branch officers that as the unidentified aircraft hovered overhead at a very low altitude, he developed sudden and out of character thoughts "of suicide, which [Dalloway] is unable to explain" (Special Branch, 1973).

It should also be noted that Special Branch was heavily involved in the investigation of numerous other events with UFO/helicopter overtones attached to them, not just in 1973, but into 1974, too.

Now it's time to take a trip across the Atlantic to the site of yet another death of undeniably suspicious proportions, one also linked with secret, government work.

Getting to the Heart of the Mystery

Pat Price was a deeply gifted remote-viewer who, in 1973, was enlisted into a program overseen by the CIA's Office of Technical Services and its Office of Research and Development. The reason: to psychically spy on the Soviets, and just about any and every potential enemy of the United States. Price proved his worth when, also in 1973, and while remote-viewing a "vacation property"—as part of a test-experiment—he also managed to psychically identify a classified installation run by the National Security Agency, much to the consternation of NSA officials when they were informed. The CIA prepared a summary report on Price's remote-viewing of the NSA facility that makes for notable reading. It states, in part:

"Pat Price, who had no military or intelligence background, provided a list of project titles associated with current and past activities including one of extreme sensitivity. Also, the codename of the site was provided. Other information concerning the physical layout of the site was accurate" (Kress, 1977).

Pat Price also, as declassified documentation makes clear, was involved in operations to try to psychically penetrate a variety of Soviet embassies and Libyan military facilities, particularly so throughout much of 1974. There was something else, too: Price became obsessed with the idea that there were hostile aliens living deep within Alaska's gigantic Mount Hayes. Interestingly, Price, having extensively remote-viewed the mountain and its interior, said the aliens were, outwardly at least, very human-like in appearance, aside from minor differences in their eyes, although their internal organs differed to significant degrees. Disturbingly, Price claimed the aliens used "thought transfer for motor control of us," and were "responsible for strange activity and malfunction of U.S. and Soviet space objects" (Schnabel, 1997). Price also came to believe he had uncovered evidence of *three more* alien installations: one beneath Mount Zicl, Australia; a second under Mount Inyangani, Zimbabwe; and a third below Mount Perdido in the Pyrenees Mountains, bordering France and Spain (Ibid.).

Price would undoubtedly have continued his work into the controversial domain of underground extraterrestrials had it not been for one thing that surfaced out of the blue early on the morning of July 14, 1975: a fatal heart attack. Tim Rifat, an authority on the history of the U.S. government's remote-viewing programs, says of Price's untimely death:

> It was alleged at the time that the Soviets poisoned Price. It would have been a top priority for the KGB to eliminate Price as his phenomenal remote-viewing abilities would have posed a significant danger to the USSR's paranormal warfare buildup. He may also have been the victim of an elite group of Russian psi-warriors trained to remotely kill enemies of the Soviet Union (Rifat, 2001).

The Days Leading up to Death

It is known that in the days that preceded his passing, Price had meetings in Washington, DC, with representatives of the National Security Agency and the Office of Naval Intelligence, specifically to discuss remote-viewing-themed work he was doing for both of them. From there, Price flew to Salt Lake City, Utah, where he visited with his son for several hours, then took a flight to Las Vegas, Nevada. The purpose was to have a friend safeguard a collection of documents should anything happen to Price while he was in Las Vegas. And if anything did happen, that same friend was to hand the papers over to the people who ran the remote-viewing program on which Price worked. Price arrived in Sin City during the late afternoon of July 13 and caught a cab to the Stardust Hotel. As he approached the desk to check in, Price collided with another man, something that, at the time, Price gave no real thought to. Very soon afterward, however, Price began to feel distinctly unwell. Weirder still, while dining with friends that night, Price announced that on the previous evening, while he was still in DC, someone slipped something into his coffee. That Price saw them doing it, however, led him to avoid drinking from the cup—which was probably very wise of him.

At about 5:00 a.m. the following morning, Price phoned his friend. He (Price) had been feeling ill all night, and things were getting worse: He was having trouble breathing, had cramps throughout much of his back and stomach, and, when the friend arrived, was noticeably perspiring. For an hour or so, Price's friend debated on whether or not a doctor should be called, but finally decided to go ahead. By this time, however, it was already too late. Price suddenly started to convulse and stopped breathing. Although paramedics were quickly on the scene, it was to no avail: Price's heart was briefly restarted, but he expired in mere minutes and was formally pronounced dead at a nearby hospital.

Concoctions That Kill

So, who or what really killed Pat Price? Certainly he did have heart disease, which makes it not impossible that his death was just a tragic and innocent one. There are, however, factors that suggest otherwise. For example, there were the concerns Price made to his friend about something untoward happening to him. There was also the matter of someone dropping who knows what into Price's coffee the night before he flew to Las Vegas. And then there was the man who collided with Price in the lobby of the Stardust Hotel in Las Vegas. This latter issue brings very much to mind the notorious death of a man named Georgi Markov, in London, in 1978.

A Bulgarian writer who was deeply critical of the iron-fisted regime in his home country, Markov defected to the West, eventually settling in London, after first spending time with his brother in Italy. For the Bulgarian police and intelligence services, Markov was a man they wanted gone, and particularly so when his profile and denunciation of the Bulgarian government increased, now that he was safely in the West. Markov didn't remain safe for long, however.

On the morning of September 11, 1978, Markov was headed to the headquarters of the BBC, where he worked. He crossed the Waterloo Bridge, which spans the River Thames, and was waiting for a bus when a man behind him got a little bit too close for comfort. It appeared that the man had lost his balance and, as he fell to the ground directly behind Markov, his umbrella stabbed Markov in the leg. The man quickly grabbed the umbrella and vanished into the London crowds. This was no accident, however. With his leg stinging, Markov made his way to work, and told his friends and colleagues of the strange encounter.

In just a few hours, Markov developed a major fever, and he died three days later from the effects of ricin poisoning—ricin being a toxic protein found in castor oil plant seeds. An autopsy revealed the presence of a small pellet in Markov's leg, exactly where the "accidental" stabbing occurred. Although the culprit has never been formally identified and charged, fingers—even those of Scotland Yard—point in the direction of the former Soviet Union's KGB and the secret police of the Bulgarian government, possibly working in tandem with each other.

Is it feasible that that collision in the Stardust Hotel in Las Vegas was actually an all-too-similar situation—one that was directly responsible for the sickly feeling that soon overcame Pat Price and that ultimately claimed his life? Very possibly, yes. And if Price, like Georgi Markov, had been autopsied, we might have a firm answer to that question. Sadly, we don't.

There is another possibility, too: that Price's death by heart attack was prompted by even stranger means.

Murder by Microwave and Psychic Phenomena

In Chapter 7 of this book, on the subject of the controversial death in 1959 of Morris K. Jessup, I referenced a March 1976 report titled "Biological Effects of Electromagnetic Radiation (Radiowaves and Microwaves) Eurasian Communist Countries," which was prepared for the Defense Intelligence Agency (DIA) by Ronald L. Adams and Dr. R.A. Williams of the U.S. Army's Medical Intelligence and Information Agency. The document is made notable, and deeply relevant to the death of Pat Price, because it makes significant mention of how a heart attack can be induced via the use of directed, microwave technology.

In a section of the document titled "Cardiovascular System," Adams and Williams note:

> Heavy emphasis has been placed on investigations involving electromagnetic radiation on the cardiovascular system. Effects on hemodynamics include blood pressure variations and cardiac arrhythmias.... Comparison of a group of engineers and administrative officials who were exposed to microwaves for a period of years and an unexposed control group revealed a significantly higher incidence of coronary disease.... Exposure may, therefore, promote an earlier onset of cardiovascular disease in susceptible individuals (Adams and Williams, 1976).

And let's not forget that this particular document deals with the use of microwaves from the perspective of utilizing them as *weapons* against targeted individuals. But the real icing on the cake comes in the form of a 1978 document, also prepared for the Defense Intelligence Agency, but this time by the U.S. Air Force's Foreign Technology Division (FTD) at Wright-Patterson Air Force Base (Dayton, Ohio), in 1978—the FTD having had longstanding involvement in the investigation of UFO reports. Its title is "Paraphsyics R&D—Warsaw Pact," and it is an in-depth study of the Warsaw Pact's extensive research into such issues as psychic phenomena, ESP, mind-reading and, rather notably, the use of paranormal powers to provoke a heart attack.

The one person who, more than any other, caught the attention of the DIA and the FTD on this matter was Gennadiy Aleksandrovich Sergeyev, a doctor of technical services at the Leningrad-based Institute of Physiology. One of the most gifted psychics that Sergeyev worked with was a woman named Nina Kulagina. It was during the course of their work together, specifically in 1970, that Sergeyev came to realize not just how amazing Kulagina's talents were, but how potentially deadly they could be, too.

The FTD noted in its report that, on one occasion, "Kulagina attempted to increase the heart rate of a skeptical physician" ("Paraphsyics R&D— Warsaw Pact," 1978). She did far more than that, as the documentation makes abundantly clear: "Electroencephalogram, electrocardiogram, and other parameters were measured," which revealed that "within 1 minute after the experiment began," the heart activity of the physician "reached dangerous levels, and the experiment was terminated" (Ibid.). The entire issue was considered to be a "serious intelligence problem" (Ibid.) No doubt about that.

What all of this demonstrates is that both in the United States and the former USSR, research was well underway, years before Price died, to try to determine how psychic phenomena and microwaves could be used to affect heart rhythms, and possibly even to a fatal degree, by inducing a devastating heart attack. Coupled with the possibility that someone may have slipped something into Price's coffee a day or so before his death, and not forgetting that curious collision in the lobby of the Stardust Hotel— and also the possibility that the aliens of Mount Hayes, Mount Ziel, Mount Inyangani, and Mount Perdido wanted him gone too, before he psychically uncovered even more of their underground network—it might be argued that not only were the odds stacked against Price, but he really didn't stand a chance in Hell.

CHAPTER 11
A DEADLY DISK IN THE DESERT

Secret Files and a UFO Down

In July 1993, a lengthy, and undeniably controversial, document was mailed anonymously to a U.S.–based UFO researcher named Elaine Douglas. It was titled "Research Findings on the Chihuahua Disk Crash" and was dated March 23, 1992. Whoever Douglas's insider source was, he or she appears to have had access to extraordinary, and highly classified, information on not just UFOs, but on human fatalities resulting from direct exposure to the flying saucer phenomenon. As to why Douglas, specifically, should have been on the receiving end of the report, there is an intriguing possibility.

In 1993, the year in which she received the report, Douglas was the Washington, D.C. representative of a public group called Operation Right to Know (ORtK), a deeply proactive body that, at the time, was lobbying the U.S. government to release its UFO files—as in *all* of them, even the highly classified ones. ORtK was thrust into the limelight, by the local media, when its staff organized a highly visible picket-march in the heart of D.C. in July 1993, the very same month Douglas obtained the illuminating document. Perhaps there were sympathetic insiders whose attention was caught by the near-unique activity then going down in the nation's capital. And, just perhaps, one of those insiders decided to secretly single out Douglas to be the one person who would get to know at least *some* of the truth behind the UFO phenomenon. The document begins:

> On 25 Aug. 74, at 2207 hrs., U.S. Air Defense radar detected an unknown approaching U.S. airspace from the Gulf of Mexico. Originally the object was tracked at 2,200 (2530 mph) knots on a bearing of 325 degrees and at an altitude of 75,000 feet, a course that would intercept U.S. territory about forty miles southwest of Corpus Christi, Texas. After approximately sixty seconds of observation, at a position 155 miles southeast of Corpus Christi, the object simultaneously decelerated to approximately 1700 (1955 mph) knots, turned to a heading of 290 degrees, and began a slow descent ("Research Findings on the Chihuahua Disk Crash," 1992).

Shortly after the craft was detected by U.S. authorities, a full-blown air defense alert was secretly initiated. Before any form of aerial interception of the unknown vehicle could be scrambled, however, it suddenly turned on a course that was destined to take it away from U.S. territory and toward Mexico. Indeed, it entered Mexican airspace approximately 40 miles south of Brownsville, Texas. American military radar personnel tracked the object for approximately 500 miles, to a point near the 18th-century town of Coyame, in the state of Chihuahua, not far from the U.S. border. There it suddenly disappeared from the radar screens. Apparently, staff at additional military facilities was also monitoring the situation, as is evidenced by the fact that further data surfaced, which filled in the blanks of the opening minutes of the otherworldly affair.

Continuing with the story, Douglas's confidante said that during the course of its flight over Mexican airspace, the object leveled off at approximately 45,000 feet, then descended to around 20,000 feet. The descent was in what were described as "level steps," rather than in a smooth curve or straight line, and each level was maintained for approximately five minutes (Ibid.). The author of the report then noted: "The object was tracked by two different military radar installations. It would have been within range of Brownsville civilian radar, but it is assumed that no civilian radar detected the object due to a lack of any such reports" (Ibid.).

The actual point of disappearance from the radar screens was over what was described as a barren and sparsely populated area of northern Mexico. At first, wrote Douglas's informant, it was assumed that the object had merely descended below the radar's horizon. Although a careful watch of the radar screens was duly maintained, the UFO was not tracked again. As will soon become apparent, there is a very good reason for the disappearance of the craft.

At first, Douglas's source continued, it was assumed that the object had possibly been a meteor, chiefly as a result of its high speed and descending flight path. Deeply problematic with such a theory, however, is the fact that, though meteors do normally travel at high speeds, they descend in smooth arcs, and certainly not in step-by-step motion. And, as if it really needs to be said, meteors most assuredly do not make sudden, 35-degree changes to their courses. Clearly, something deeply strange and enigmatic was afoot in the night skies of Mexico.

Shortly thereafter, there was a dramatic development in the story, as the document makes abundantly clear:

> Fifty-two minutes after the disappearance, civilian radio traffic indicated that a civilian aircraft had gone down in that area. But it was clear that the missing aircraft had departed El Paso International with a destination of Mexico City, and could not, therefore, have been the object tracked over the Gulf of Mexico. It was noted, however, that they both disappeared in the same area and at the same time (Ibid.).

Mayhem in Mexico

A sensational and extraordinary picture was coming together: There appeared to have been a violent, mid-air collision between a definitive UFO and a small aircraft of distinctly terrestrial origins. Elaine Douglas was told this:

With daylight the next day, Mexican authorities began a search for the missing plane. Approximately 1035 hrs there came a radio report that wreckage from the missing plane had been spotted from the air. Almost immediately came a report of a second plane on the ground a few miles from the first. A few minutes later an additional report stated that the second 'plane' was circular shaped and apparently in one piece although damaged. A few minutes after that the Mexican military clamped a radio silence on all search efforts (Ibid.).

Douglas's source confided in her that, by this time, all of the inter-cepted, and duly recorded, radio transmissions of the Mexicans were secretly being forwarded to senior personnel in the CIA for analysis, and possibly to two more agencies, too, although this latter point remained unconfirmed. The CIA immediately swung into action. A team—comprised of highly trained personnel—was put together with one goal in mind: to recover the strange, circular object that had collided with the small air-craft, which obviously happened to be in the same area at just about the worst time possible.

It was made very clear to the recovery team that, if all attempts at diplomacy failed, the unknown craft was to be taken out of the hands of the Mexican military by force. And, if it really came down to it and there was no choice left available, by *deadly* force. There was a very good reason for this, as Douglas's contact explained to her: "Requests were initiated at the highest levels between the United States and Mexican governments that the U.S. recovery team be allowed onto Mexican territory to 'assist.' These requests were met with professed ignorance and a flat refusal of any cooperation" (Ibid.). For the Mexicans, and quite understandably, it was a case of what happens in Mexico stays in Mexico.

Matters then progressed very quickly:

By 2100 hrs, 26 Aug. 74, the recovery team had assembled and been staged at Fort Bliss [Texas]. Several helicopters were flown in from some unknown source and assembled in a secured area. These helicopters were painted a neutral sand color and bore no markings. Eyewitness indicates that there were three smaller craft, very possibly UH1 Hueys from the description. There was also a larger helicopter, possibly a Sea Stallion. Personnel from this team remained with their craft and had no contact with other Fort Bliss personnel (Ibid.).

Deaths in the Desert

From what Elaine Douglas was told, it appears that such was the concern over what had occurred, U.S. spy satellites were vectored to photograph the crash site, and, just for good measure, American spy planes were ordered to take high-resolution photos of the impact area, too. It was then that the CIA realized there had been a major development: Although the site of the crash of both the aircraft and the UFO was located with ease, to the deep concern of U.S. Intelligence was the fact that they were now no longer in sight. Both had vanished. The reason why soon became apparent.

As the pilots of the spy planes scoured the area, they noticed in the distance a convoy comprised of military flatbed trucks, jeeps, and a variety of additional vehicles. There was, however, something very curious about the convoy: It was totally unmoving. On the one hand, this was a relief to the CIA; if a confrontation between American and Mexican forces did occur, then the fact that, for some odd reason, the convoy had come to a grinding halt in the desert, made it much easier for the U.S. military to move in, surround the Mexican personnel, secure the area, and take hold of the unknown aerial vehicle.

Nevertheless, the CIA knew that the Mexicans were hardly likely to give up such a prized find without a fight, and there was a profound worry that matters might descend into not just an American-Mexican confrontation and standoff, but an outright firefight of fatal proportions and an international incident. An "alien Alamo," one might justifiably say. Fortunately, such a potentially calamitous situation did not come to pass—but, as it transpires, for highly worrying reasons.

Orders were given to the pilots of the reconnaissance aircraft to make low-level passes of the Mexican convoy, as a means to try to figure out why all of the vehicles had inexplicably stopped in the desert, rather than heading directly, and speedily, to the nearest military installation. The answer quickly became clear. As Douglas's source revealed, the aerial photographs taken by the crews "showed all trucks and jeeps stopped, some with open doors, and two human bodies lying on the ground beside two vehicles. The decision was immediately made to launch the recovery team but the actual launching was held up for the arrival of additional equipment and two additional personnel. It was not until 1438 hrs. that the helicopters departed Fort Bliss" (Ibid.).

Not long after, a team of U.S. military personnel and a group of experts in the field of biological warfare were on the ground. Douglas was told:

> All convoy personnel were dead, most within the trucks. Some recovery team members, dressed in bio-protection suits, reconfigured the straps holding the object on the flatbed truck; then attached them to a cargo cable from the Sea Stallion. By 1714 hrs the recovered object was on its way to U.S. territory. Before leaving the convoy site, members of the recovery team gathered together the Mexican vehicles and bodies, then destroyed all with high explosives. This included the pieces of the civilian light plane which had been involved in the mid-air collision. At 1746 hrs the Hueys departed (Ibid.).

Later that evening, the entire team finally made its way across the border and back into the United States. Their final destination was soon in sight: a point in the Davis Mountains, which are located in western Texas, about 25 miles northeast of the small town of Valentine. On landing, the group was told to sit tight and await further instructions. Finally, those instructions came through: A specially converted truck was on its way to a mountainous area in the vicinity of the town of Van Horn. Still under cover of darkness, the helicopter crews made one last flight, to where they rendezvoused with the truck. Douglas's contact outlined the next part of the story:

The recovered disk was transferred to a truck large enough to handle it and capable of being sealed totally. Some of the personnel from the Hueys transferred to the convoy. All helicopters then returned to their original bases for decontamination procedures. The convoy continued non-stop, using back roads and smaller highways, and staying away from cities. The destination of the convoy report-edly was Atlanta, Georgia. Here the hard evidence thins out. One unconfirmed report says the disk was eventually transferred to Wright-Patterson A.F. Base. Another says that the disk was either transferred after that to another unnamed base, or was taken directly to this unknown base directly from Atlanta (Ibid.).

As for the UFO itself, it was described to Douglas as being around 16 feet in diameter, and having a weight close to 1,500 pounds. It was con-vex on both upper and lower surfaces to the same degree, and completely lacking in doors or windows. The thickness was slightly less than 5 feet. As for its color, it was silver, very much like polished steel. No form of propulsion was readily visible. *Very* visible, however, were two areas of the rim that showed significant damage, including an irregular hole, approx-imately 12 inches in diameter, with "indented material around it" (Ibid.). The other damage was described as being a 2-foot-wide "dent," which had clearly been caused by the impact with the unfortunate aircraft, which was referred to as being "almost totally destroyed" (Ibid.).

The Centers for Disease Control Connection

On the most worrying part of the whole affair—namely, the matter of how and why the entire Mexican recovery team was found dead—we have the following:

Unfortunately, what caused the deaths of the Mexican recovery team is not known. Speculation ranges from a chemical released from the disk as a result of the dam-age, to a microbiological agent. There are no indications of death or illness by any of the recovery team. It would not have been illogical for the recovery team to have taken one of the bodies back with them for analysis. But there is no indication of that having happened. Perhaps they did not have adequate means of transporting what might have been a biologically contaminated body (Ibid.).

In conclusion, Elaine Douglas was advised that "...the facts that are known have been gathered from two eye witness accounts, documentation illegally copied, and a partially destroyed document. This was done in 1978 by a person who is now dead. Only in February of this year did the notes and documents come into the hands of our group" (Ibid.). Precisely who, or what, "our group" was or still is, was never made clear. We can, at least, assume that the person who chose to confide in Douglas had deep connections to the military, but was seemingly linked to a group of fellow personnel that did not agree with the U.S. government's policy of widespread secrecy when it came to the UFO controversy.

There is, however, one more point that is worthy of note: the location to which the disk was apparently taken—namely Atlanta, Georgia. It transpires, somewhat intriguingly, that Atlanta is home to the headquarters of the Centers for Disease Control (CDC). The CDC is at the forefront of helping to lessen, and ultimately stop, any and all threats posed by hostile forces that may wish to unleash deadly viruses upon the United States and its people. Category A viruses, for the CDC, are considered to be the most serious of all.

They are those specific viruses that, says the CDC, "can be easily spread or transmitted from person to person," that "result in high death rates and have the potential for major public health impact," that "might cause panic and social disruption," and that would "require special action for public health preparedness" ("Bioterrorism Agents/Diseases (by Category)"). It practically goes without saying that all four of those criteria which fall into the CDC's "Category A" could more than easily apply to the outbreak of a virus of alien origins, one with a connection to a crashed UFO event.

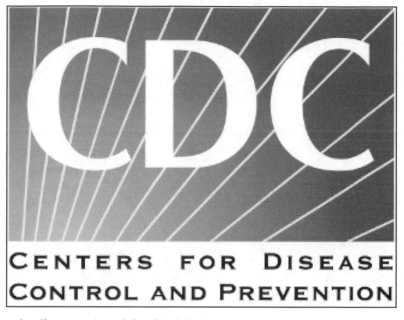

UFOs, deadly viruses, and the CDC (U.S. Government, 2006).

Moreover, and by the CDC's very own admission, its work is "a critical component of overall U.S. national security" (Ibid.). The U.S. government most assuredly recognizes the critical importance of the CDC from that very same national security perspective. Currently, the CDC receives yearly funding of approximately $1.3 billion to "build and strengthen national preparedness for public health emergencies caused by natural, accidental, or intentional events" (Ibid.). It also works closely with the Department of Homeland Security, and with FEMA, the Federal Emergency Management Agency.

Considering that it was suspected by U.S. authorities that the team of Mexican military personnel was killed by a microbiological agent, and possibly even a fast-acting, extraterrestrial virus, the CDC in Atlanta would have been the absolute ideal place to transfer any infected corpses for careful examination and secret autopsy, if such were recovered. Once again, we see how, and why, the UFO phenomenon is a profoundly deadly one.

CHAPTER 12
UFOs AND HUMAN MUTILATIONS

Close Encounters of the Slicing and Dicing Kind

A strange and terrifying new phenomenon reared its foul head all across the United States in the mid-1960s. It is a phenomenon that can most accurately be described in two words: animal mutilations. For almost half a century, cattle, horses, and pigs have been found dead under deeply horrific circumstances. Eyes, internal organs, lips, tongues, blood, and sexual organs are typically targeted by the mysterious mutilators. But this is most assuredly not the work of hungry and savage wolves, coyotes, or mountain lions. Rather, the killing of the animals, and the attendant removal of bodily materials, always appears to be undertaken with surprising stealth, speed, and the benefit of advanced technology.

Theories for who, or what, the mutilators might be, and the matter of their motivations, are many and varied. They include:

⇒ Extraterrestrials that are using the purloined body parts in obscene experimentation of near-*Frankenstein*-like proportions.

⇒ Government personnel who are concerned by the possibility of new and lethal "Mad Cow"–like viruses entering the food chain.

⇒ Occult-based groups engaged in infernal rites and rituals of the sacrificial kind.

⇒ Military bodies that are covertly testing sophisticated biological-warfare technology on the unfortunate animals.

Regardless of the answer (or, perhaps, the *answers*) it's important to note that there is one particular aspect of this eerie enigma that very seldom gets addressed. This is deeply puzzling, because it is arguably far more significant and serious in nature than anything involving animals could ever be: It's the phenomenon of *human* mutilations.

Welcome to the Jungle

One of the most graphically nightmarish accounts that falls into the human mutilation category came from the late Leonard Stringfield, who, during the Second World War and its immediate aftermath, was attached to the U.S. 5th Air Force in a military-intelligence capacity. On August 28, 1945, and while flying in a Curtiss C46 *Commando* aircraft over Iwo Jima, Japan, at around 10,000 feet, Stringfield and the rest of the crew encountered a trio of teardrop-shaped UFOs that adversely affected the engines and navigation equipment of the aircraft, and almost resulted in violent death for all aboard. Fortunately, as the UFOs exited the area, the pilot was able to regain control of the aircraft and disaster was averted. This experience led Stringfield to devote much of his post-military life to unraveling the complexities of the UFO mystery. Although Stringfield chiefly focused his investigations on reports of crashed UFOs held by the U.S. government, it was a case of a very different nature—one that was brought to Stringfield's attention in 1989—that really stands out in the fatal stakes.

Stringfield's source for the story was a high-ranking military officer described as a wholly reliable individual who Stringfield had then known for several years. After some careful consideration, Stringfield's informant decided to come clean on a shocking event that reportedly occurred somewhere in Cambodia during the Vietnam War. It was April 1972, and an elite and highly trained U.S. Army special-ops-type group, of which Stringfield's confidante was a member, found itself involved in nothing less than a violent and grisly confrontation with a group of extraterrestrials that can best, and accurately, be called cosmic butchers.

When the event occurred, the team was making its careful and quiet way through a heavily forested area of Cambodia, to a specific area near the border of Vietnam. The location in question, it was suspected, was home to a North Vietnamese listening post that was actively intercepting classified U.S. military radio-based messages. Terminating the enemy outfit with extreme prejudice was very much the order of the day. Fate stepped in, however, and the order was never fulfilled. What did come to pass, however, was something far worse than anything the team could possibly have envisaged, even during the most violent of all confrontations with North Vietnamese troops.

Meat-Packers From the Stars

As the unit reached a clearing, they were shocked to see sitting on the jungle floor, and directly in front of them, a highly reflective, circular-shaped machine, with a diameter of around 50 feet and tripod-like landing gear. So brilliantly reflective was the craft that it practically acted as a mirror. Curiously, a deep hum emanated from the futuristic device, provoking feelings of disorientation and nausea in some of the team. But that was not all: Around the vehicle were a number of humanoid figures that could only be described as extraterrestrial; their heads were large and hairless, and their wraparound eyes were utterly black. But it was not so much the appearance of the creatures that numbed the team to its core. Rather, it was what the aliens were doing—namely, systematically loading a number of human body parts and naked human corpses into large metallic bins and sealing them tight. The bodies, said Stringfield's informant, were a mixture of what were considered to be Vietnamese and white and black American troops.

To its credit, the U.S. team kept its composure, quietly positioned themselves among the surrounding foliage for cover, and wasted no time in opening fire on the bug-eyed body-snatchers. For the most part, this proved to be utterly futile, as the creatures appeared to be protected by suits that were near-armor-plated. Nevertheless, one was said to have been killed by friendly fire and three by head shots. One of the troops reportedly lost his life, and several of the men were significantly burned by a ray-type of weapon that was fired from within the UFO. With one death and several severe injuries, the team quickly backed away, at which point the aliens—seeing their chance—did likewise and ran for their craft. An opening appeared in its side and the crew scrambled aboard, while hauling the bins inside, too. The doorway suddenly closed and the UFO took to the skies, accelerating at an incredible speed after it cleared the lush, jungle canopy. In seconds, it was out of sight.

The traumatized team quickly radioed the camp at which they were stationed and explained the deadly nature of what had just taken place. It seems that the higher echelons of the military may have had previous knowledge of potentially similar events: When the facts were relayed, the uninjured members of the team were quickly flown to a military base in South Vietnam, where they were interrogated by a mysterious group of individuals that was comprised of intelligence agents, rather than of military personnel. The surviving members of the unit were warned of the serious, and possibly deadly, consequences that could result if they dared to go public with what they saw and knew. Some of the men, Stringfield was advised, were subjected to deep-hypnosis techniques that allowed for cover stories to be created. The reason: to help bury the real memories deep in the subconscious.

There can be little doubt that this particular account is a highly sensational one. It's also an account that sounds like it might have come straight out of *Predator,* the 1987 movie starring Arnold Schwarzenegger, in which a hostile alien hunts down U.S. military personnel in the jungles of Central America. Nevertheless, Leonard Stringfield stood by the story, and by his high-ranking source, until his dying day in 1994. And it's a story that is far from being a solitary one.

"These Mutilations of Cattle Are Only a Forerunner for Later Mutilations of Human Beings"

Only one year after the deadly encounter in Cambodia previously described reportedly occurred, the FBI began to systematically and quietly investigate the animal mutilation mystery—which undeniably reached its height in the mid-1970s. As well as collecting and studying a wealth of official reports submitted by law enforcement officials in both New Mexico and Colorado, the FBI also made it its business to get hold of just about every newspaper and magazine article that had been published on the subject up until that time. This included a lengthy article that appeared in a 1976 edition of *Oui* magazine. Notably, the FBI has, under the terms of the Freedom of Information Act, declassified its files on animal mutilations, including its photocopy of the *Oui* article.

The article was hit upon by FBI agents at the Bureau's Springfield, Illinois, office, who quickly forwarded a copy on to FBI headquarters in Washington, D.C. The special agent in charge at Springfield specifically highlighted to HQ—but for reasons unknown *outside* of the FBI— that the article contained theories that "these mutilations of cattle are only a forerunner for later mutilations of human beings." (See image "Mutilation of Two Cows," 1976, shown on page 134). And it's even more interesting to note that the FBI-human mutilation connections do not end there.

"We Belong to Something"

A longtime UFO researcher and investigator, and a former co-editor of the newsstand publication *UFO Magazine,* Don Ecker is both a Vietnam veteran and a police investigator. Back in the 1980s, Ecker began to dig into the human mutilation angle of the UFO phenomenon. One of the stories that Ecker uncovered was particularly disturbing: In 1979, somewhere between Bliss and Jerome, Idaho, a pair of hunters came across the corpse of a man missing both lips, one ear, and the sexual organs. That's to say, this was not the work of a wild animal, such as a bear: The procedures had been performed with surgical expertise.

An FBI document on controversial human mutilations (FBI, 1976).

Ten years later, such infernal things were still afoot: In 1989, Ecker learned, staff at various mortuaries in the New York area found themselves immersed in deeply troubling events: Someone, or *something,* had been breaking into the buildings and stealing human body parts. Typically, the break-ins occurred in the early hours of the morning and involved the theft of the genitalia, the thyroid glands, the eyes, and the stomachs of the stored, deceased individuals. Such was the widespread scale of the events that a hasty cover-up was put into place, as part of a concerted effort to prevent the story from surfacing and provoking public panic.

During the course of his investigations, Ecker contacted a friend, Scot, a police detective who had, over the years, taken part in the investigation of a number of cattle mutilation incidents. Ecker explained to Scot that he had an interest in the human-mutes issue and asked Scot if there was any way in which he might be able to lend assistance, such as possibly by making inquiries with the National Crime Information Center (NCIC). Scot agreed to help—to the extent that he was able. It so happens that the NCIC, which was established in 1967 as a centralized database for information on criminal activity across the United States, is coordinated by the FBI's Criminal Justice Information Services Division.

Very pleased by Scot's willingness to help out, Ecker sent his detective friend various data he had uncovered on alleged human mutilations and sat back to see what might develop. Well, something *did* develop, but it may not have been what Ecker was hoping for or anticipating. Only a few days later, Scot was back in touch with Ecker: "Someone is sitting on something, big as Hell" (Ecker, 1989). Not only that, a contact in the Department of Justice advised Scot that the whole matter was one best avoided, if one knew what was good for oneself.

On this matter of cold-hearted extraterrestrials using us—the human race—in cattle-like style, it's perhaps wise to close with the words of the late Charles Fort, noted author of a number of acclaimed books on strange phenomena, including *Wild Talents, Lo!,* and *New Lands*. He famously wrote, "I think we're property. I should say we belong to something" (Fort, 2004). Fort may have been closer to the terrible truth than he ever could have imagined.

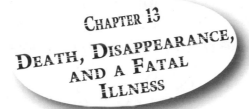

Chapter 13
Death, Disappearance, and a Fatal Illness

An Atomic Encounter

Eleven years after Edward Bryant's untimely ending (see Chapter 9), strange events were unfolding in England that ended in chillingly similar fashion. It was, rather appropriately, shortly before the witching hour on the night of March 17, 1978, when Kenneth Edwards, one year shy of 40 at the time and seemingly in very good health, was driving to his home in the town of Warrington, in the county of Cheshire. As well as being a pleasant place, one with a population close to a quarter of a million, Warrington is noted for something else: its links to the secret world of advanced weaponry and atomic energy–based research. Much of that research was, for years, undertaken at Risley, a neighborhood located in north Warrington.

During the Second World War, a Royal Ordnance Factory (ROF) was constructed at Risley to both produce and protect a dizzying variety of weapons and arms with which to help defeat the Nazis. Such was the extent of the work undertaken at Risley, almost two dozen underground bunkers were built to contain the ever-growing mass of munitions. British Nuclear Fuels, Ltd. had its headquarters based at Risley until 2003. Atomic weapons research was clandestinely carried out in the area for decades.

Throughout the Cold War the area was carefully monitored by British Intelligence, to ensure that its strategic facilities did not fall foul of Soviet penetration. And it was against this backdrop of matters secret and sensitive that something strange and deadly occurred to Kenneth Edwards.

As Edwards drove past one of the atomic energy facilities, his attention was caught by something decidedly out of place: a veritable Goliath of a figure heading down an embankment (adjacent to the facility) in a strange, jerky, robotic fashion. Edwards came to a screeching halt, shocked by the sight of such a gigantic humanoid in his very midst, one easily seven feet in height.

Shock and astonishment were soon replaced by outright terror: The bizarre figure, dressed in some sort of outfit that resembled the protection suits used by the staff at the nuclear facility, walked into the middle of the road, turned to face Edwards, and suddenly beamed a pair of thin white lights from its eyes, directly into Edwards's van! A panicked Edwards immediately felt dizzy, disoriented, and temporarily paralyzed. Just as bad, a sudden and stifling heat filled the interior, which made the skin on Edwards's hands start to blister. Then his radio fried. It was all that Edwards could do to stare, in full-blown fear, as the monstrous form then made its way to a secure fence that surrounded the facility's fire-station and passed right through it, specter-style, and vanished into the night and darkened, nearby woods.

When he finally gathered his wits together, Edwards floored the accelerator and headed home. Only adding to his consternation was the discovery that he was missing somewhere in the region of an hour of time. What had happened in the period of time, Edwards had no idea. Nevertheless, his wife, Barbara, could clearly see that her husband was in a deep state of shock. And then there was another development: Edwards asked Barbara to take him to the local police station. Interestingly, the two responding cops that sat and listened to Edwards's bizarre tale chose to drive him back to the site, where they were confronted by no less than 10 security personnel—*all* of who did a careful search of the grounds of the facility, but *none* of who were willing to enter the woods where the mysterious giant disappeared. Whatever dissuaded them from doing so was never made clear. Things were far from over, however.

Illness and Death

Post–March 17, 1978, Edwards had several additional encounters at the site, one of which involved a second sighting of the silver figure; the others were focused on eerie feelings experienced by Edwards that led him, finally, to never again take that route home. It wasn't long before the local and national media latched onto the story, briefly thrusting Edwards into a limelight of the kind he most surely did not want or need. The worst was still to come, however. Less than a year after his unearthly encounter, Edwards fell sick with cancer—specifically of the kidneys. It soon spread, and Edwards was not long for this plane of existence.

It might be said that Kenneth Edwards's encounter was with an entity born on a world far away—and, just maybe, that was exactly the case. On the other hand, let's not forget that the tall terror was seen on the fringes of a highly secret, British government facility. It was even wearing an outfit not unlike a typical hazmat-style suit, the type routinely worn by workers in the nuclear industry. Then there were the findings of Jenny Randles and Peter Hough, two UFO researchers who were determined to get to the heart of the mystery. Although the pair didn't solve the puzzle, they did learn that certain strange and classified experimentation—of a sensory deprivation nature, no less—was afoot pretty much right next door to where Kenneth Edwards's silver man appeared. In view of this, is it feasible that Edwards became the unwitting victim of some unscrupulous and reckless project, one not unlike the so-called microwave incident that claimed the life of Edward Bryant in 1967?

After all, what is more likely: a deadly alien on the loose, or a heavily protected employee of some clandestine agency testing a new and deadly weapon on an unsuspecting member of the British public? If it happened to Edward Bryant in the 1960s, could it not have happened to Kenneth Edwards in 1978?

A Flying Saucer, an Exploded Aircraft, and the FBI

In July 1978, a mysterious death, reportedly caused by a UFO 11 years earlier, almost turned upside down the life of an American UFO researcher named Robert Todd. Several months previously, the well-known UFO authority, Stanton T. Friedman, was quietly approached by a man who claimed knowledge of a UFO incident in March 1967 that very possibly resulted in a fatal outcome for a military pilot. That this was far removed from being an innocuous light in the sky-type report ensured Friedman asked for more details. He got them.

The man in question, at the time, worked for the 6947th Security Squadron at Homestead Air Force Base, in Florida. The 6947th was a body of significance and importance: It was an arm of the U.S. Air Force Security Service (AFSS), and part of its job was to eavesdrop on the conversations of Cuban military pilots. Since the Cuban Missile Crisis had brought the world to the absolute brink of global nuclear war only five years earlier, the work of the 6947th was imperative from a national security perspective.

On the day in question, the team was scanning the airwaves, when they picked up a fascinating, but also alarming, conversation. Cuban air defense staff was screaming that an unknown target was approaching the coast of Cuba, from the northeast, at a height of about 33,000 feet, and a speed of close to 700 mph. The Cubans wasted no time at all in dispatching a pair of MIG-21 fighters that had been supplied by the Soviet Union. As they got within a couple of miles of the target, the team leader was able to make a visual sighting. Whatever it was, it was no normal aircraft: Circular in shape, and highly reflective, it was, by definition, a UFO.

When attempts made to contact the pilot of the UFO went unanswered—if the craft even had a pilot—the flight leader was ordered to blast the vehicle out of the sky. It was not a wise move. The pilot succeeded in locking in on the UFO's signature with his radar and was ready to let loose his impressive arsenal when, suddenly, the MIG exploded in midair. Very curiously, the aircraft did not burst into flames, but, according to the pilot of the second plane, seemed to disintegrate in the sky. There was no hope for the pilot. The UFO did not hang around. It soon reached a height of almost 100,000 feet and was lost as it headed off toward South America. Given that the work of the U.S. Air Force Security Service fell under the auspices of the Big Brother–like National Security Agency, the NSA's cleared staff was fully briefed on the deadly nature of the aerial encounter. And now we jump forward to 1978.

A Knock at the Door

Robert Todd, who died in 2007 at the age of 53, was someone who used the Freedom of Information Act (FOIA) to a near-obsessive degree in his efforts to try to understand what the U.S. government really knew about UFOs. He came upon the Cuban story in a roundabout fashion: Stanton T. Friedman shared the details with a man named Bob Pratt, a writer for the *National Enquirer.* Pratt, having a deep interest in UFOs, then had Todd take a look at the story, as a means to try to get some form of verification. Pratt got more than verification: He had none other than the FBI banging on his front door.

From early to mid-1978, Todd filed FOIA request upon FOIA request with numerous arms of the U.S. government, military, and intelligence community, as he sought to gain a full picture of the Cuban incident. All of the replies came back negative. The CIA, however, did have one bit of advice for Todd: Its staff suggested that he should think about contacting the Cubans directly to get their opinion on the matter. Whereas this might, initially, be perceived as a helpful act, it may actually have been intended to plunge Todd into the turbulent depths of scalding hot water—which is *exactly* what happened.

Todd advised both the Air Force and the NSA that, because they were apparently unwilling to help him in his quest for the truth about the 1967 event over Cuba, he would take the CIA's advice and go directly to the Cubans for the answers. Behind the scenes, Todd had mightily pissed off someone.

Exactly two weeks after he tipped off the Air Force and the NSA to his next step, Todd got a visit. It was around dinnertime and Todd, who lived with his parents, was upstairs when there was a knock on the door. His mother answered it, only to be confronted by two suit-wearing feds, who asked for Todd. As he came downstairs, Todd already guessed what it was about. In no time at all, Todd was briefed on the government's then-current espionage laws, as well as on the possible sentence for getting Uncle Sam in a serious state of flux: life in prison or even death. Todd also learned, during the classic good cop–bad cop grilling, that the decision to have the FBI look into Todd's activities was the NSA's.

There then followed a question and answer session in which the FBI agents wanted to know all about the circumstances of, and the background concerning, his involvement in the Cuban story, who originally uncovered the details, and with whom they had been shared. Despite the fact that one of the agents claimed that the bulk of the story was "bullshit," a discussion of the possibility that the family's phone was bugged caused both agents to smile knowingly (Fawcett and Greenwood, 1984). They soon left.

Ultimately, Todd did not fall foul of the U.S. government's espionage laws, and the FBI, NSA, and Air Force did their utmost to say nothing else at all about the events of March 1967, or why it was of such concern to them. UFO researchers Lawrence Fawcett and Barry Greenwood offered that the Todd affair strongly suggested the Cuban case was all too real. They also postulated that the FBI's visit to Todd was designed purely for "the purpose of scaring him out of his wits" (Ibid.). It worked.

A UFO Appears and an Aircraft Vanishes

Quite possibly the most dramatic UFO-based event of 1978 occurred on the evening of October 21 of that year. Frederick Valentich was, at the time, 20 years of age and a pilot, having secured a private pilot license in 1977, at the age of just 19. On the night in question, Valentich departed from Moorabin Airport, located in Melbourne, the capital city of the Australian state of Victoria. His aircraft: a Cessna 182. Valentich's plan was to fly to King Island, Victoria, a distance of just under 130 miles, and over the Bass Strait. Official records show that Valentich took to the skies at 6:19 p.m., on a clear night and with only light winds in evidence. Everything should have gone smoothly. As fate would have it, the evening was anything *but* a smooth one. Approximately three quarters of an hour into the flight, something very strange happened, something that ultimately resulted in Valentich vanishing—forever.

As the official papers show, Valentich contacted staff at Melbourne and inquired if there was "any known traffic below five thousand [feet]?" The answer was negative. Valentich was puzzled, as he was sure he could see what he first described as "a large aircraft." When the Melbourne Flight Service Unit Coordinator asked Valentich exactly what kind of aircraft, Valentich could only state that he was unable to confirm its type, except that it seemed to be illuminated by four bright lights. Things soon went from puzzling to downright sinister, as Valentich's words make very clear: "Melbourne, it's approaching me now from due east towards me. It seems to me that he's playing some sort of game. He's flying over me two to three times at speeds I could not identify" (Australian Department of Transport, 1978).

An extract from the Australian Department of Transport's file on missing pilot Frederick Valentich (Australian Department of Transportation, 1978).

When asked to do so by Melbourne, Valentich confirmed his height at 4,500 feet, adding that "as it's flying past, it's a long shape." A stressed Valentich continued: "Melbourne, it seems like it's chasing me. What I'm doing now is orbiting and the thing is just orbiting on top of me, also. It's got a green light and sort of metallic. It's all shiny." Then, the strange craft seemingly vanished in an instant, but not for long: "Approaching from the southwest. The engine is rough idling" (Ibid.).

Concerned staff at Melbourne asked: "What are your intentions" (Ibid.)?

"My intentions are, er, to go to King Island. Er, Melbourne, that strange aircraft is hovering on top of me again," replied Valentich (Ibid.). The last known words ever spoken by the young pilot were: "It is hovering and it's not an aircraft" (Ibid). They were words followed by seconds of a strange, unidentifiable noise.

Not only was Valentich never seen again, neither was his aircraft. And, despite an extensive search that was launched practically immediately, and that carefully scanned both the skies above and the waters below, no adequate answer to the mystery was ever found. A detailed study of the unfortunately scant facts undertaken by Australia's Department of Transportation also drew a blank.

What, Exactly, Happened to Frederick Valentich?

The bizarre nature of Valentich's disappearance, the repeated references to the strange and unidentifiable nature of the unidentified craft—and not forgetting its ability to hover directly over Valentich's Cessna—have all led many a UFO researcher to conclude that Valentich and his plane were either destroyed by some form of vehicle from another world, or that both pilot and aircraft were the victims of a cosmic kidnapping.

Theories soon abounded for what might have happened. There was the idea that Valentich staged his disappearance, as a means to make a new, fresh start somewhere else, possibly under an assumed name. Certainly, Valentich gave conflicting stories concerning the reason for his flight to King Island. Staff at Melbourne Airport understood that the purpose of Valentich's flight was to pick up a number of people and bring them back to Melbourne. Valentich told his girlfriend he was going to collect a large order of crawfish. Then there was the possibility of suicide. Although the family was adamant that Valentich had everything to live for, and certainly nothing to die for, it didn't stop such a theory from circulating and being considered. Also considered was the scenario of Valentich becoming disastrously disoriented and plummeting into the Bass Strait.

In 2012, the Department of Transport's official file on the disappearance of Frederick Valentich was finally released into the public domain. It ran in excess of 300 pages, excited students of the UFO phenomenon, and gave at least some comfort to the Valentich family (if nothing clsc, it showed that a determined effort had been made to get to the bottom of the mystery), but that was all. There was still no answer to what really happened to Frederick Valentich on the night of October 21, 1978. And there still isn't.

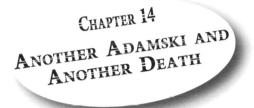

CHAPTER 14
ANOTHER ADAMSKI AND ANOTHER DEATH

A Corpse on a Coal Stack

In an earlier chapter we saw how, in 1965, a British man named Edward Bryant became embroiled in a UFO event that, in a strange and roundabout fashion, involved the infamous Contactee George Adamski. It was an event that unfortunately proved to be fatal for Bryant. As you will recall, Bryant's encounter occurred just one day after Adamski's death. Moreover, his alleged aliens made a couched reference to the Adamski-sounding "Yamski," and they even commented on "Des" and "Les," which is perceived by many UFO investigators as a direct reference to Desmond Leslie, Adamski's co-author on their mammoth-selling 1953 book, *Flying Saucers Have Landed* (Bowen, 1969).

All of this takes on greater significance when we learn that Adamski—the name, if not the man himself—features in yet *another* baffling UFO-themed death, this one *also* in England, but years later. It's an affair that started with a suspected murder that still mystifies to this very day and that ended in a close encounter of just about the most amazing variety possible. It started on a summer's day in 1980—June 11, to be specific. The location was the Yorkshire, England, town of Todmorden, a 17th-century locale with, today, a population of less than 15,000.

For Trevor Parker, the day began as a normal one. It most assuredly did not end that way, however. Parker's father owned a coal yard in town and, while in the yard and as a torrential, afternoon downpour soaked Todmorden and its people to their core, young Parker discovered something shocking: a dead body lying on a 10-foot-high stack of coal. But that was not all: The head of the deceased man displayed a significantly sized burn. And, rather oddly, though the dead man was dressed in his jacket and trousers, he was lacking a shirt, the zipper on his trousers was undone, his shoes were tied strangely and had seemingly been placed on his feet by someone else, and the buttons of his jacket were pushed through the wrong holes. Parker quickly called the emergency services.

A Man Named Adamski

It did not take long at all for the police to identify the victim. His name was Zigmund Adamski and, although Polish by birth, he hailed from Tingley, Yorkshire, where he worked at the Lofthouse mining colliery. Adding to the mystery, however, was the fact that when Adamski's body was found, he had already been missing for five days, although the condition of the corpse made it clear he had certainly not been dead for all of those five days. Plus, the distance from Tingley to Todmorden—by road—was about 27 miles. How, or even why, Adamski ended up in Todmorden was equally perplexing. A major investigation was immediately launched, which is not surprising, given that murder was hardly a daily event in Todmorden.

Deeper inquiries by the police allowed them to piece together at least a part of the picture of Adamski's movements prior to his disappearance, as well as collect background data on the man. Adamski and his wife, Lottie, had lived in Todmorden for decades, they were a devoted couple, and no one could understand why someone might have wanted Adamski dead. His health, however, was not good at the time he vanished: he suffered from both lung disease and heart disease—the latter, the coroner determined, being the cause of Adamski's death.

All that the police were able to determine was that on June 6, Adamski and a couple of relatives over from Poland, who were in England to attend the wedding of Adamski's goddaughter the very next day, had lunch in Tingley, after which Adamski set off to run a few chores. And that's where the trail ran not just cold, but downright frozen. This did not, however, deter the police from diligently following every conceivable lead. Unfortunately, the more the authorities dug into the matter of Adamski's death, the more mysterious and confusing everything became.

Earlier on the day Adamski's body was found, Trevor Parker had been working in the coal yard, and he was absolutely adamant that the body was not there at that time. This begged important questions: How, and why on earth, did someone choose the middle of the day to move a dead body? Why did they select, of all places possible, a hardly quiet coal yard in town? Why not dump Adamski's body on the wilds of the Yorkshire Moors, late at night and well away from any potentially prying eyes? And how, exactly, was the corpse placed atop a 10-foot-high stack of coal at all? Such an action would have surely required the strength of at least two men, if not three, to haul a male, adult corpse to such a height and carefully position it on the coal stack.

The next step was to see what the autopsy of Adamski's body had revealed. The state of the corpse suggested strongly that Adamski died only a couple of hours before Parker found him—which led the police to believe the decision to place the body on the coal stack was a hasty, last-minute one. As for that curious burn on Adamski's head, well, that was another puzzle entirely. Egg-shaped, it appeared that someone had applied some form of cream designed to alleviate the effects of a burn. But, the burn was not caused by exposure to an open flame. The coroner deduced that the cause was due to something of a decidedly corrosive nature.

The autopsy gave no indication as to where Adamski had been—or had been kept—in the days that preceded his death, although he did not appear to have been mistreated in any way, the burn aside. Adamski certainly hadn't gone without food, and an estimation was made he had shaved up until around the day before he died. Although the ultimate conclusion was death by natural causes, the mystery of Adamski's whereabouts prior to his final moments, not to forget the matter of how his body got to the coal stack, led even the police to strongly suspect there was far more to the story than anyone knew—the suspected killer, or killers, aside of course.

Though the very name, Adamski, and his attendant mysterious burn, caused a few intrigued UFO researchers to take at least a cursory note of the affair when it first surfaced, it was later in 1980 when the mystery of Zigmund Adamski's death was taken to whole new levels of intrigue.

Policing the UFO

One of the two police officers who responded to Trevor Parker's emergency phone call was Constable Alan Godfrey. It was Godfrey, specifically, who noted the odd way in which Adamski was dressed—or, very likely, had been dressed by someone else. Most notable of all, however, in November 1980, five months after he was plunged into the investigation of Adamski's death, Alan Godfrey himself had a UFO encounter of fantastic proportions. It was also very much a Contactee-style encounter of the type reported by the *other* Adamski—George—back in the 1950s, given that Godfrey's alien was not of the small, black-eyed variety that are so often reported today, but of a very human type and dressed in a flowing, gown-like outfit.

Todmorden, England: the site of a mysterious death and abduction by aliens (Loh93, 2006).

The strange, and quite possibly unearthly, events began during the pre-dawn hours of Saturday, November 29, 1980. Godfrey was on patrol in Todmorden at the time, his night shift having commenced some hours earlier and due to finish about 6:00 a.m. Such is the relative quiet nature of life in Todmorden, Godfrey's duties that Saturday did not involve apprehending burglars, chasing down muggers, or pursuing the drivers of stolen cars. For Godfrey and his colleague, much of the night was spent searching, unsuccessfully, for a missing herd of cattle. An hour or so before he was due to go off duty, and having failed to find the cows, Godfrey headed for the police station. At the last minute, however, he decided to have one last look for the cows. He did so alone; his colleague remained at the station.

It was while traveling along the Burnley Road, a road that was still dark, due to both the time of the morning and the inclement, rainy weather, that Godfrey had what was without doubt the shock of his life. As he headed to the corner of Ferney Lee Road, Godfrey was mystified by something sitting in the road, some distance in front of him. As he stared ahead, puzzled and slightly concerned, Godfrey's mind tried to place things into a down to earth context. For a few moments, he mused on the possibility that what he was seeing was nothing stranger than a typical English double-decker bus, albeit one stationary at a precarious angle on the road. As Godfrey closed in, however, he could see that the bus was actually nothing of the sort. It was, instead, a significantly sized egg-shaped object, with underside illumination that seemed to shimmer as it rotated at a fast rate, and that appeared to have windows running along its circumference.

Rather disturbingly, Godfrey's VHF and UHF communication devices failed to work in close proximity to the object. He was all alone, in utter darkness, and unable to contact his colleagues at the police station to let them know what was going on. Nevertheless, and to his credit, Godfrey kept a cool head and quickly sketched the craft, as it appeared before him. Then, without warning, Godfrey was hit by a blinding light that clearly caused a significant degree of disorientation, because his next recollection was of driving the police car, about 300 feet beyond where he had seen the strange craft. Godfrey was in two minds as to whether or not he should report the details of what had just occurred. Slightly concerned over what his friends and colleagues in the force might think, he held off from doing so until the following morning, when he finally decided to come clean. An official report was made, and that was that—or so Godfrey thought.

In the days, weeks, and months that followed, Godfrey experienced a number of unusual dreams and fragmentary memories, all of which suggested his conscious recollections of what happened during the early hours of that fateful Saturday in November 1980 did not tell the whole story. The time finally came, in August 1981, when Godfrey decided it was time to try to figure out what *really* happened on that dark morning all those months earlier. He elected to be hypnotized, as a means to get to the heart of the puzzle.

Seeking the Answers in an Altered State

Subjected to a number of hypnotic regressions, in which he was plunged into significantly traumatized states, Godfrey told a remarkable story: The bright flash of light—that he remembered consciously—apparently incapacitated his police car and bathed him in its eerie glow. He was then levitated into what can only be described as a UFO, via a doorway in its side, and into a room of fairly small proportions and, oddly, a room that was *carpeted*. The next stage of the encounter saw Godfrey placed onto a bed of sorts, one of a leather-like appearance. Then something amazing happened.

Godfrey was confronted by a very human-looking being that looked like he had stepped out of *The Lord of the Rings*: He had a long, hooked nose and a full beard, and was dressed in a white gown. The smiling man, who identified himself as Yosef, was not alone, however. A group of robot-like entities, around 3 1/2 feet tall, were in attendance, and assisted in the placing of metallic bands on Godfrey's head and limbs. There are hints of coded messages given to Godfrey, as well as the possibility of medical examinations and, very intriguingly, fragmented memories of childhood encounters with alien entities and mysterious balls of light seen floating in his bedroom. As for how Godfrey was returned to his police car, hypnosis failed to shed any light on the matter.

Those of a skeptical mindset might suggest that although Godfrey may have seen *something* on the Burnley Road, the hypnosis might have provoked not memories but a vivid story borne out of Godfrey's subconscious, albeit certainly not deliberately or maliciously. To his credit, though Godfrey stands 100 percent by his story of having seen a UFO in the road—one that, as a result of its size, would have prevented him driving past it, even if he had tried to do so—he admits he cannot say for certain that the hypnosis did not bring forth fantasies from deep within the recesses of his mind. It must be stressed, however, that anyone who has watched the videos of Godfrey's initial regression to November 29, 1980—a regression that was undertaken by a psychiatrist named Dr. Joseph Jaffe—cannot fail to see the emotional pain and terror on Godfrey's face as he describes his time spent aboard the strange craft.

The Deadliest Dog of All

There is one other aspect of Alan Godfrey's encounter that I have left until now. While under hypnosis, Godfrey blurted out that, while on the UFO, he saw "a bloody dog." When the hypnotherapist asked Godfrey to describe the dog, he said: "Well, I think it's a dog. Horrible. Just looks like a dog. Like the size of an Alsatian [Author's note: British terminology for a German Shepherd]." It, Godfrey added: "just sat there." When asked about the dog's color, Godfrey replied with just one word: "black" (Randles, 1983).

It transpires that this was not the first time that Godfrey had had an association to a hound of the paranormal kind. While they were still girlfriend and boyfriend, his wife had seen what can only be described as a ghostly black Labrador. Also, in the 1960s, and while driving near Todmorden in the early hours of one particular morning, what appeared to be a woman with a large black dog stepped out in front of Godfrey's vehicle, causing him to slam on the brakes. Not only did a frantic search reveal no sign of either woman or dog, Godfrey suffered a mystifying time loss of around two hours.

It must be stressed that the British Isles are absolutely *filled*—and have been for centuries—with reports of phantom black dogs, most of which are perceived as omens of death and creatures linked to the afterlife. Bob Trubshaw, an authority on the subject, notes that these particular hounds, with eyes that glow "red as burning coals," are "part of a world-wide belief that dogs are sensitive to spirits and the approach of death, and keep watch over the dead and dying. North European and Scandinavian myths dating back to the Iron Age depict dogs as corpse eaters and the guardians of the roads to hell" (Trubshaw, 2005).

How curious that just five months after having played a significant role in the investigation of the very weird death of Zigmund Adamski—one that has long been tied to the flying saucer phenomenon—Alan Godfrey had a UFO encounter that involved the sighting of a creature so widely associated across the United Kingdom with the realm of the dead.

Saucers and the Occult

As interesting as all of this is, it begs an important question: Why would ghostly black dogs with blazing red eyes and an overriding association with death have a connection to the UFO phenomenon in the first place? Well, if the phenomenon has extraterrestrial origins, they likely wouldn't. But, what if the phenomenon *isn't* extraterrestrial? Within the field of UFO research, there is an entire sub-culture that believes the flying saucer enigma is definitely demonic in origin and nature. So the theory goes: The Devil's minions manifest before us in the guise of aliens to lure us into a kind of satanic deception, one designed to bring people over to the dark side, by ingeniously enticing them with an extraterrestrial encounter that is actually nothing, at all, of the sort.

Before you rule out such a controversial theory, it's worth noting that Todmorden has in its midst what are called the Gabriel Hounds. Researcher Chris Huff notes of this particular brand of marauding phantom black dog that has haunted the old, windswept moors around town for centuries and taken the lives of fear-filled local folk: "They are perceived to fly down the Cliviger Gorge and vanish into the ground. It is only since the advent of Christianity in the north that they have been associated with the angel Gabriel, the spirit of truth, and also of fire and lightning" (Huff).

There is one other thing, too: Todmorden is home to Blackheath Barrow, a Bronze Age site, the 100-foot circular remains of which can just about be seen to this day, if one looks closely at the terrain of what is now the town's golf club. Also known as Frying Pan Circle and Roman Barrow, it's a site where numerous cremated remains of the ancients have been found in old urns. It's also a place where it was believed the dead showed themselves when certain old rites and rituals of Bronze Age man were practiced. J. Lawson Russell, a man with a passion for the mysterious places of the past, noted of Blackheath Barrow that funeral rites were regularly carried out at the site.

Another intriguing belief is that although Blackheath Barrow was utilized by Bronze Age people, it was created, long before, by the fairy folk. They were diminutive entities, known for their magical powers, their predilection for stealing babies, and their ability to provoke missing time in those who crossed their paths—all of which are facets of today's so-called alien abduction lore. On this same path, one night, in 1982, none other than the wife of the landowner of Blackheath Barrow saw a strange ball of light near the old Bronze Age creation. Things then became decidedly hazy; her next recollection was of waking up on the grassy fringes of the barrow, and with absolutely no indication of how she got there. And, lest we forget, Alan Godfrey's November 1980 abduction and subsequent hypnosis revealed that he, too, had a close encounter of the glowing ball of light kind as a child and also experienced a period of missing time while aboard a UFO.

So what we have here with Todmorden is not just your average, old English town, after all. This is a place where magical and mysterious death has dominated for countless centuries, particularly in relation to phantom black dog encounters—a phenomenon Alan Godfrey was acutely aware of and linked to. We also have an old Bronze Age structure, one allegedly built by supernatural dwarfs, where strange aerial lights have been seen and where a woman experienced missing time at the dawning of the 1980s.

It cannot be said with any degree of certainty that all of this talk of supernatural death, lethal hounds of the paranormal kind, and the weirder aspects of the Alan Godfrey affair make it more likely than not that Zigmund Adamski's death was due to the actions of non-human entities— whether from the stars or from some hellish realm. All of the above *does* demonstrate one thing, however: Todmorden is, and has been for time immemorial, a place steeped in matters relative to death of the most mysterious kind.

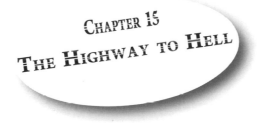

CHAPTER 15
THE HIGHWAY TO HELL

Conspiracy in the Lone Star State

Imagine the scene: It's late one December evening in 1980 and you are driving down a long stretch of tree-enveloped road in southeast Texas. Your attention is suddenly drawn to a strange light in the sky. You stare at it intently and in puzzled, and slightly alarmed, fashion. No wonder, as this is not a normal light in the slightest. Rather than appearing like the kind of illumination one would expect to see on an aircraft, this light appears to be nothing less than a mass of fire in the sky. In an alarmingly quick time, the light descends perilously close to the ground—as in barely 25 feet above the surface of the road—at which point you're now able to make out the shape of a strange, diamond-like object, one with a blue row of lights, and flames wildly emanating from its underside.

By now both amazed and terrified, you bring the car to a sudden halt. As a Christian, your first thought is not that you're seeing a UFO, but the second coming of Jesus. Wrong: The son of God, it's not. It's far more like the Devil himself. Then matters really heat up, as in literally. The temperature inside the car becomes unbearable, to the point where you are forced to get out—quickly. And it's just as hot outside. Although you are more than 100 feet from the strange device, its overpowering, torturous heat makes even touching the door handle of your car a hazardous task. Now that you're outside of the vehicle, you can tell that the device is making a strange bleeping noise. A distress signal, maybe? Suddenly, the fiery object begins to move, albeit in cautious and noticeably shaky fashion.

You jump back into the car and start to follow it, slowly and deliberately. As you do so, you see what appears to be about two dozen, double-rotor military helicopters closing in on the object, possibly shadowing it or escorting it to destinations unknown. Finally, and just under an hour later, you decide that the wisest thing you can do is to get the hell out of Dodge and head for home—which is exactly what you do.

Alien Exposure

If all of this sounds like science-fiction, you would be wrong—dead wrong, in fact. It's an all-too-real encounter that affected and traumatized a trio of witnesses more than three decades ago, and that possibly even led to the death of one of them. The victims of the event—for they were surely that—were Vickie Landrum; her 7-year-old grandson, Colby; and a friend of Vickie's, Betty Cash. The location was Cleveland-Huffman Road at Huffman, Texas (not too far from Houston), and the time when all hell broke loose was just about 9:00 p.m. The three had been out eating on the night in question. The dinner was good. The dessert, however, proved to be terrifying. The aftermath was even worse.

Whereas most witnesses to a significant UFO encounter would likely concede that the event left an emotional or psychological mark on them, for Landrum, Colby, and Cash, those marks were physical—and there was nothing positive about them in the slightest. Many of the symptoms were similar to those that one might associate with a particularly bad case of food poisoning: They suffered from dehydration, severe diarrhea, headaches, incessant sickness, and an inability to keep anything liquid or solid down. But, whereas food poisoning generally clears up in a day or so, this was not the case here. In Betty Cash's case, the symptoms not only persisted but increased and mutated to the point where they became downright terrifying and finally lethal—quite possibly because she was the one that had the closest exposure to the craft.

Within just days of the encounter, Cash, to her horror, broke out in sores, all across her body. On top of that, her hair began to fall out. And we're not talking about a few strands here and there: Entire patches of her head became exposed as the days progressed. It was, by then, time to hit the emergency room. Altogether, Cash spent nearly a month in hospital in the aftermath of the exposure to the vehicle from, well, *somewhere*. Cash was scared, and the doctors were baffled. Then news came that perhaps Cash was anticipating, but most assuredly didn't want to hear: There was a possibility, and certainly a suspicion on the part of some of the medical personnel who examined Cash, that she had been exposed to dangerous levels of radiation. Only a few weeks earlier, Cash had been celebrating Christmas with her family. Now, however, her life was in turmoil and upheaval.

Looking for Answers

That the UFO was being escorted by a squadron of what were clearly military helicopters, which Cash was later able to almost conclusively iden-tify as double-rotor Boeing CH-47 Chinooks, Cash decided that the wis-est course of action was to contact the world of officialdom and raise hell. Given the close proximity to the Houston Space Center, Cash contacted NASA in February 1981, shortly after her release from hospital. Cash wasted no time in coming straight to the point, and demanded to know if NASA had been flying something weird and hazardous in the vicinity of Huffman on December 29, 1980. No one should be surprised that the response was a decisive: no. NASA did offer some help, however. Its staff referred Cash to the project manager for Space Shuttle Flight Operations. Though that might seem a strange decision for NASA to have taken, it was not. The project manager was also a keen UFO enthusiast and, at the time, the deputy director of the world's biggest flying saucer research organiza-tion, the Mutual UFO Network (MUFON). His name: John Schuessler.

It was largely thanks to Schuessler's diligence and digging that the events of December 29, 1980, did not go away anytime soon. Schuessler made numerous inquiries as he sought to figure out what it was that really caused so much terror and ill health on that fateful night. He went knocking on official door after official door, but it was all to no avail.

The military flatly, and on the record, claimed no knowledge of the UFO, and denied having *any* CH-47 Chinooks in the skies of Huffman in late December 1980, never mind in excess of 20 of them. On top of that, the U.S. Army maintained it didn't even have the ability to get so many helicopters into the air that night without leaving at least some form of paper trail, of which there was none at all—at least, none that was publicly accessible. As matters progressed (if "progressed" is the appropriate word to use), Betty Cash's health took a drastic turn for the worse: Alopecia and skin rashes were nothing compared to the breast cancer she developed, and that finally resulted in a double mastectomy.

Going to Court

Attempts to have the military held accountable in some fashion finally stalled, too. Although Betty Cash and Vickie Landrum secured an attorney to try to get some form of financial compensation for the traumatic ordeal that all three witnesses had been put through—compensation in the figure of $20 million—the suit was thrown out of court in August 1986. The reason for the dismissal: Whatever the true nature of the unidentified, wobbling, fiery object, no evidence was brought before the judge that proved the craft originated with some arm of U.S. officialdom. And, if it wasn't ours, said Judge Ross Sterling, then there were no grounds upon which the government, or the military, could be prosecuted for damages. Outrageously, as a result of the lack of evidence suggesting the military knew far more than it was saying, the judge wouldn't even begin to hear what Landrum and Cash's lawyers had to say.

Ultimately, the matter of what truly happened down in southeast Texas two days before the end of 1980 was never resolved: Betty Cash and Vicki Landrum stood by their story (while young Colby preferred to remain in the background), officialdom steadfastly denied it, and John Schuessler continued to try to open yet further doors to the truth. Today, more than 30 years down the line, that truth has still not surfaced. As for poor Betty Cash, there was no positive outcome; her health never recovered and, in somewhat eerie fashion, the Grim Reaper took her *exactly* 18 years after that night near the town of Huffman.

An Insider Spills the Beans

On the matter of what it was that caused so much damage and destruction to the lives of three innocent individuals, a fairly strong case has been made that the UFO was some form of highly advanced vehicle of the military, even if such a theory has consistently had scorn poured on it by the U.S. government. Before we get to the matter of the unknown craft itself, there is the far-from-insignificant matter of that veritable armada of helicopters.

Mystery helicopters—or "black helicopters" and "phantom helicopters," as they have infamously become known—are a staple part of Ufology. They are very often seen at so-called cattle-mutilation sites, in relation to surveillance of those who claim to have been abducted by aliens, and at alleged UFO crash sites. Collectively, this has given rise to the theory that some clandestine arm of the military is operating a helicopter-based, quick-response unit, one that is designed to deal with UFO-themed matters of a serious and national security–affecting nature. It's a theory that may well be right on target.

Tom Adams spent much of the 1970s and 1980s digging very deeply in the matter of unidentified helicopter links to the UFO and cattle-mutilation issues. In doing so, he stumbled upon the testimony of "Tony," a helicopter pilot based at Fort Hood, Texas. Late one night, in December 1980, a night that Tony distinctly recalled was after Christmas Day but before the new year, he and a number of his colleagues were ordered to fly a covert mission to what we now know to be around Huffman, Texas. They were advised to keep a look out for an "unusual aircraft," one that the pilots of the choppers would be required to try and keep as close to the ground as possible (Adams, 1991). That even meant the precarious possibility of having a crew actually hover directly above the craft and carefully use the weight of the helicopter to force it downward, to the ground. Tony added that when they reached the area and caught sight of the aerial device (which wasn't hard, as it was "throwing off sparks like a 4th of July sparkler"), they shadowed it from anywhere between 7 to 10 miles, after which they were suddenly ordered to abort the mission (Ibid.).

Days later, Tony learned further details from some of his colleagues. The craft was by definition a UFO, but it wasn't made by bug-eyed aliens from some far away galaxy: It was all the work of Uncle Sam, an experimental aircraft that experienced problems and that led to the need for an emergency team to hit the area with extreme speed. As for the reason the mission was aborted, whatever the nature of the malfunction, it was ultimately rectified, something that allowed for its controllers to complete their mission—which was possibly a test flight of the futuristic-looking vehicle, one that may even have been nuclear-powered.

On a very similar path, Betty Cash's physician, Dr. Brian McClelland, went on record as stating that he had a source who advised him the exotic aircraft was an experimental, nuclear-powered craft known as the Wasp II. A near-identical claim to that of Tony was made by a shadowy, military source known as "Falcon" on a 1988 television show, *UFO Cover-Up? Live.*

Is it, therefore, possible that Betty Cash, who unwisely chose to walk toward the craft as it hovered precariously in front of her, was exposed to deadly radiation at the time of her encounter—something that caused so much sickness, hair loss and, finally, a fatal dose of cancer? It's not impossible. However, researcher Brad Sparks prefers another, but no less intriguing possibility. He notes that if Cash really was bathed in so much radiation that it led to blistering, loss of hair, nausea, and vomiting, then she should have died within weeks, rather than having had ongoing, post-event medical problems for years. Sparks has offered the theory that Cash, the closest one to the UFO, was possibly exposed to a chemical agent, many of which mimic the effects of ionizing radiation. Either way, the end result was the same: As a result of her close encounter of quite possibly a very earthly kind, Cash's health suffered not just adversely but, finally, to a fatal degree.

The Rendlesham Forest Angle

There is one final matter to address on the curious saga of Betty Cash and Vickie and Colby Landrum, and it relates to the time frame: late December 1980. Coincidentally, or maybe *not* coincidentally *at all*, at the exact same time that tumultuous events of an unknown nature were exploding across Huffman, Texas, they were doing likewise in an area of English woodland called Rendlesham Forest.

Between the nights of December 26 and 29, 1980, multiple, extraordinary UFO events occurred within the woods in question that involved military personnel from the nearby Royal Air Force stations of Bentwaters and Woodbridge. Since that now-long-gone period, countless U.S. Air Force personnel, who were stationed in the area at the time, have spoken out regarding their knowledge of a small, triangular-shaped object that was seen maneuvering in the forest. Others described seeing in the dark woods almost ghostly, extraterrestrial-type beings of short size and with eerie, feline-like eyes. Strange and unknown lights were seen dancing around the night skies, circling both the forest and the twin military facilities. There were stories that the amazing movements of the UFOs were caught on radar. And there was even hushed talk of those military personnel involved in the incident being silenced by ominous Men in Black–style characters.

But that's not all: The date issue aside, there are a couple more connections between the Rendlesham case and the events that occurred in Texas during the very same time frame. The theory that the UFO encountered by Betty Cash, Vickie Landrum, and Vickie's grandson, Colby, was radioactive is made even more notable by the fact that elevated radiation readings were picked up in none other than Rendlesham Forest at the height of the mystery—something confirmed in a January 1981 memo written by Deputy Base Commander Colonel Charles Halt. In 1997, I interviewed Nick Pope, a now-retired employee of the British Ministry of Defense who, between 1991 and 1994, worked in one of several offices of the MoD that studied UFO reports. Pope told me at the time:

> I've made no secret of the fact that I've tried to reopen the investigation into the Rendlesham Forest incident. I took the raw data from Colonel Halt's memo and gave it to the Defense Radiological Protection Service, and they came back and said, words to the effect: "What the bloody hell happened there?" The radiation was ten times normal. That was sufficient to confirm that there was something very strange at the landing site (Redfern, 1997).

And there's more to come.

The 67th Aerospace Rescue and Recovery Squadron: A Connection?

In the same way that all of the evidence seems to suggest the large number of helicopters in evidence at Huffman amounted to an emergency-response team, it so happens that RAF Woodbridge was home to a very similar quick-response unit, too. It was the 67th Aerospace Rescue and Recovery Squadron of the U.S. Air Force which, as Captain John E. Boyle, chief of the Public Affairs Office at RAF Bentwaters told me in 1988, "provided stand-by rescue coverage for the American space flights" (Boyle, 1988).

Captain Boyle continued:

> Of course, they were never needed to provide emergency rescue actions, but at the time, the unit was trained and available to rescue astronauts with their HH-53 and HC-130 aircraft. In early 1988, the 67 AARS was re-designated as part of the 39th Special Operations Wing, their primary mission changing from that of rescue to supporting U.S. Special Operations forces. Their secondary mission remains that of search and rescue and they would provide any assistance necessary in future space missions (Ibid.).

Today, the unit goes by the moniker of the 67th Special Operations Squadron and operates out of a British Royal Air Force base called Mildenhall, in the English county of Suffolk. Rather notably, its staff has close links to the NASA's Lyndon B. Johnson Space Center in Houston, Texas—just a short drive to the town of Huffman where three lives were affected to a terrible degree in December 1980.

On this same issue, UFO researcher Jenny Randles asks a thought-provoking question: If something strange, unearthly or domestic, came down in Rendlesham Forest on the first night of the encounters, December 26, 1980, "could it have been shipped to the Texas coast in four days" (Randles, 1998)? She notes that "as Huffman is so close to the coast near Galveston, the object could have been picked up from an aircraft carrier and ferried to its destination by helicopters belonging to some highly covert military operation" (Ibid.).

Although some might suggest that such a thing is far too fantastic for words, let's look at the facts. Both the Huffman and the Rendlesham events occurred at the same time. The Cash-Landrum case had an emergency-response component in the form of a squadron of helicopters, albeit admittedly one from who knows where. RAF Woodbridge had its very own such unit: the 67th Aerospace Rescue and Recovery Squadron, which had ties to the Houston, Texas-based Lyndon B. Johnson Space Center, which, at a distance of only 47 miles from Huffman, makes matters all the more intriguing.

The chances of us knowing what it was that Betty Cash, Vickie Landrum, and Colby Landrum encountered in December 1980 on a darkened stretch of Texas road diminish just about as quickly as the years roll by. Perhaps the craft was indeed a highly classified device of the U.S. military, one that briefly malfunctioned—for Betty Cash, in particular, at just about the deadliest time and place conceivably possible. On the other hand, maybe the secret aircraft angle was introduced to cover up something else: the recovery of a craft of non-human origins that came down in Rendlesham Forest, England, and that was secretly and hastily shipped to the United States.

In December 1980, in Texas, a squadron of Boeing CH-47 Chinook helicopters was seen escorting a malfunctioning UFO (U.S. Army, 1950s).

If the latter scenario is the correct one, then just perhaps it was not the craft itself that was malfunctioning, but a Chinook helicopter that was carrying the UFO beneath its fuselage. Given that it was late at night, and on a dark and heavily wooded road, the possibility of the helicopter crew having to make an emergency landing, by first carefully lowering the craft to the ground, might well have been perceived as the device landing under its own power and volition. Only when it became apparent to the helicopter crew that the driver and the passengers of an approaching car had witnessed the near-calamity did they hastily take to the skies and try and find a more secure and hidden place to land.

Somewhere, in this admittedly confusing mass of data, the truth is likely to exist, regardless of whether or not we will ultimately be able to prove it as such. Of only one thing can we be sure: Yet again, a UFO encounter of noteworthy and astounding proportions proved to be life-ending.

Chapter 16
Star Wars of the Deadly Kind

SDI: Guarding the Skies

From the mid-1980s to the early 1990s, a significant number of individuals working for a leading defense contractor in the United Kingdom died under highly suspicious and dubious circumstances. That many of them—chiefly computer programmers and scientists—were attached to projects allied to U.S. President Ronald Reagan's famous Strategic Defense Initiative (SDI) program of the 1980s, has led to an astonishing theory: Those whose lives came to sudden ends were killed by a deadly foe of unearthly proportions. To be sure, it sounds like wild science fiction. Quite possibly, however, it may be equally wild science fact.

It was in March 1983 that President Reagan announced his plans to create a futuristic defense system designed to ensure the Western world remained free of nuclear attack by the Soviets. The Strategic Defense Initiative was its official title, though the project is far better known by its nickname: "Star Wars." The idea, which finally got off the ground in 1984, was a decidedly far-reaching and alternative one. Essentially, the plan involved deploying powerful laser-based weapons into the Earth's orbit that, in essence, would provide a collective shield that could skillfully and decisively destroy any incoming Soviet or Chinese nuclear weapons. The program was not just ambitious; it finally proved to be *overly* ambitious.

Ultimately, the Strategic Defense Initiative program collapsed under its own weight and a lack of adequate technology to allow it to work in the fashion that Reagan had enthusiastically envisaged. Nevertheless, it wasn't entirely abandoned: During the Clinton administration it became the Ballistic Missile Defense Organization, and is today known as the Missile Defense Agency (MDA). Although the MDA is a vital component of America's defense and security, it's a far cry from the *Star Wars*–like SDI-based imagery of hundreds of laser-firing weapon-systems positioned high above the United States. But, in its very earliest years, SDI *was* seen as a winner by many. And, as a result, that a leading British defense contractor was recruited to come on board and help develop the vital technologies that the project sorely needed.

UFOs, strange deaths, and the Strategic Defense Initiative (U.S. Government, 1985).

But was it really the Soviets that Reagan was worried about? Ever since the SDI program was announced, rumors have circulated to the effect that it was a far stranger enemy that was plaguing the mind of the president, an enemy that wasn't even human or fully understood, in terms of its origins and motivations. SDI, the theory goes, was planned to take on not an internal threat, but an *external* one: an evil, extraterrestrial empire, no less.

UFOs and Star Wars

It's a notable fact that President Reagan made a number of intriguing statements relative to the UFO phenomenon in the mid-1980s—when SDI research was at its height—and specifically from the potential threat it posed to each and every one of us. It all began in November 1985, at the Geneva Summit, when Reagan was deep in discussion with Soviet Premier

Mikhail Gorbachev. The subject: trying to find a way to reverse the arms race and decrease the threat of a global, nuclear holocaust. Formerly classified memoranda generated by the Department of Defense in 1985 tell an interesting story:

> Reagan said that while the General Secretary was speaking, he had been thinking of various problems being discussed at the talks. He said that previous to the General Secretary's remarks, he had been telling Foreign Minister Shevardnadze (who was sitting to the President's right) that if the people of the world were to find out that there was some alien life form that was going to attack the Earth approaching on Halley's Comet, then that knowledge would unite all the peoples of the world. Further, the President observed that General Secretary Gorbachev had cited a Biblical quotation, and the President is also alluding to the Bible, pointed out that Acts 16 refers to the fact that "we are all of one blood regardless of where we live on the Earth," and we should never forget that (Reagan's Extraterrestrial Fixation…, 2009).

Barely four weeks had passed before Reagan publicly raised the UFO issue yet again. This time it was before an entranced throng at Fallston High School, in Harford County, Maryland. He told the packed crowd:

> I couldn't help but—when you stop to think that we're all God's children, wherever we live in the world—I couldn't help but say to [Gorbachev] just how easy his task and mine might be if suddenly there was a threat to this world from some other species from another planet outside in the universe. We'd forget all the little local differences that we have between our countries and we would find out once and for all that we really are all human beings here on this Earth together. Well, I guess we can wait for some alien race to come down and threaten us, but I think that between us we can bring about that realization (Cameron, 2009).

And Reagan was far from done with alluding to the world that, just perhaps, there might be an extraterrestrial threat waiting in the wings to assume control of the planet. It was September 21, 1987 when, before none other than the United Nations' General Assembly, Reagan told a captivated audience:

> In our obsession with antagonisms of the moment, we often forget how much unites all the members of humanity. Perhaps we need some outside, universal threat to make us recognize this common bond. I occasionally think how quickly our differences worldwide would vanish if we were facing an alien threat from outside this world. And yet, I ask you, is not an alien force already among us? What could be more alien to the universal aspirations of our peoples than war and the threat of war? (Ibid.)

Was there really a connection between the SDI program, Reagan's comments, and deadly aliens lurking and machinating in our very midst? Although the hypothesis that Reagan's Star Wars program was designed to stave off a potential alien attack on the Earth is controversial in the extreme, it is an undeniable reality that others have made near-identical claims.

War of the Worlds

The late Colonel Philip Corso, of the U.S. Army, and someone who claimed to have worked with alien technology recovered near Roswell, New Mexico, in 1947, said that at the height of the Cold War:

> ...the military found itself fighting a two-front war, a war against the Communists who were seeking to undermine our institutions while threatening our allies and, as unbelievable as it sounds, a war against extraterrestrials, who posed an even greater threat than the Communist forces. So we used the extraterrestrials' own technology against them, feeding it out to our defense contractors and then adapting it for use in space-related defense systems (Corso and Birnes, 1997).

Corso continued, in a fashion that leaves no room for misinterpretation on his words:

> It took us until the 1980s, but in the end we were able to deploy enough of the Strategic Defense Initiative, "Star Wars," to achieve the capability of knocking down enemy satellites, killing the electronic guidance systems of incoming enemy warheads, and disabling enemy spacecraft, if we had to, to pose a threat. It was alien technology that we used: lasers, accelerated particle-beam weapons, and aircraft equipped with "Stealth" features. And in the end, we not only outlasted the Soviets and ended the Cold War, but we forced a stalemate with the extraterrestrials, who were not so invulnerable after all (Ibid.).

It must be noted that Corso has as many believers as he does disbelievers in his controversial claims. But there is one thing that goes far beyond a mere claim: When President Reagan was pushing his SDI dreams, and curiously dropping little hints and clues about dangerous extraterrestrials in our midst, the Grim Reaper came calling upon dozens of British scientists and computer experts with more than a few SDI links themselves. And most of them were employed by, or undertook contract-based work for, a company called Marconi Electronic Systems—or GEC-Marconi, and which, in 1999, was taken over by British Aerospace and is now known as BAE Systems Electronics Limited. It's a company whose research is at the forefront of cutting-edge technologies in the fields of advanced weaponry, electronics, lasers, underwater-based weapon systems, and space-satellite components.

We have already seen how, in the early 1970s, Marconi was embroiled in a couple of strange deaths with UFO connections. In the 1980s, however, it was prestigious contracts connected to Ronald Reagan's Strategic Defense Initiative that kept Marconi's personnel busy—when they weren't mysteriously dropping like flies, that is.

The Death List Begins, and Gets Bigger and Bigger

The earliest case on record that appears to tie in to the undeniably strange saga occurred in March 1982. The victim was Professor Keith

Bowden, who was then age 46. A scientist with significant computer-simulation skills, he undertook a sizeable amount of work for Marconi in the early 1980s—that is, until death unfortunately decided to make an appearance. It came in the form of a car accident in which Bowden's BMW crossed a highway and plummeted onto an old stretch of unused railway track. Then, in November 1985, the body of Jonathan Wash, who worked for the UK's British Telecom Technology Executive, an agency that had significant ties to the defense world—including Marconi's parent body, GEC—was found after he allegedly fell, or jumped, from the balcony of a hotel in Abidjan, a city in the West African country of Ivory Coast. The verdict was a straightforward suicide.

Moving ahead one year, on August 4, 1986, 24-year-old Vimal Bhagvangi Dajibhai, a computer programmer who worked at Marconi Underwater Systems, threw himself off the huge Clifton Suspension Bridge, which spans England's River Avon. The 240-plus-foot fall ensured that Dajibhai's death was inevitable. The verdict of the coroner was, as was the case with Jonathan Wash, suicide, something that deeply puzzled his family, as a result of Dajibhai's strong personality and driven ambition. Two months later, in October, Arshad Sharif—also a computer programmer and also linked to Marconi—killed himself in horrific fashion: The 26-year-old tied one end of a lengthy piece of rope around a tree, then got inside his car, tied the other end of the rope around his neck, started the engine, and hit the accelerator. Death was instantaneous.

Right around the Christmas period in 1986, Dr. John Brittan, a scientist in the British defense industry, found himself in a ditch after losing control of his car. Utterly baffled as to what had happened, Brittan remained deeply uneasy about the whole affair—but not for long: On 12 January, 1987 he, too, was dead—allegedly from self-induced carbon-monoxide poisoning in his garage. It must be said here, as an aside, that Brittan's death by carbon-monoxide poisoning, following on directly from an inexplicable car accident, *exactly* mirrors the circumstances surrounding the 1959 death in Florida of UFO researcher Morris K. Jessup. And still on the UFO issue...

Elimination of Non-Military Personnel

Coincidence or not, in October 1986—right in the middle of a cluster of Marconi deaths that spanned from August to December of that year—English UFO researcher Jenny Randles was contacted by a former British Army source ("Robert") who claimed access to highly classified U.S. military files on UFOs, crashed flying saucers, alien autopsies, and the U.S. government's most guarded UFO secrets of all. They were also files that dealt with controversial deaths in the UFO field. Such was the potential importance of the revelations, Randles and a colleague, Peter Hough, met with Robert in the town of Eccles, England, not far from where Randles was living at the time. As Randles and Hough listened intently, an amazing story tumbled out.

As Robert explained, the files in question were originally computerized and stumbled upon, a year or so earlier, by a computer specialist doing repair work at Wright-Patterson Air Force Base, in Dayton, Ohio—an installation with numerous UFO links, and the alleged resting place of more than a few crashed UFOs and preserved extraterrestrial corpses. Recognizing the significance of the papers, the man managed to print around 600 pages, which was said to have been a small portion of the overall total. The man was friends with Robert's commanding officer (CO), who was on an exchange program in the States, and secretly passed the files on to the CO, who managed to get them out of the country and to the UK. Supposedly, Robert was told, the very same computer technician died shortly afterward in a highly suspicious car accident, one blamed on drunk driving.

When I interviewed Randles about this issue, in 1997, she told me what happened next: "Robert's CO explained that he was due to take on a new position within the British Army and he needed to offload the UFO files. Was Robert the man for the job?" As it transpires, Randles explained to me, yes, Robert *was* the man for the job. After reading the mass of documentation, however, and realizing the gravity of the situation in which he now found himself—ostensibly in the illegal possession of highly classified U.S. military files—Robert quickly became a worried man—a *very* worried man (Redfern, Interview with Jenny Randles, 1997).

A planned attempt to have Robert give the papers to Randles, roughly one week after their meeting, failed miserably: At some point during the next seven days, Robert was visited by what he termed his "former employers" and taken to a military base in the south of England for interrogation. Randles outlined for me the next development: "They knew all about the six hundred pages of documentation, which they ordered him to hand over, pointing out that he had a wife and children and it was they who would suffer if he didn't" (Ibid.). Robert, fearful of the possibility that his family might be killed, did as he was told, amid a stern warning never to talk about the files again—even though he was advised that the papers amounted to nothing more than "a prank on someone's part" (Ibid.).

Those of a skeptical mind might suggest that Robert was simply a Walter Mitty–style fantasist and nothing more, and, as a result, it was inevitable that the papers would never surface. Randles's additional words to me suggest otherwise. She and Hough had the presence of mind to have Robert thoroughly checked out by a trusted contact in the British Police Force: "It turned out that what [Robert] had told us proved to be correct. The name he had given us was his real name; he lived where he said he lived; he had recently been in the Army; and his car had been registered in the area he worked in precisely the same month that his Army career had come to an end" (Ibid.).

Though the very odd, and almost Machiavellian, affair was over, one particular revelation from Robert really stuck in Randles's mind. One of the "biggest single files" in the entire collection, Randles advised me, "was one with a rather disturbing title: 'Elimination of Non-Military Personnel'" (Ibid.).

Randles continued:

> [Robert] said that this was a document discussing the ways in which witnesses who had come into possession of too much information on UFOs were silenced. And although this sounds very much like something out of a spy film, from his detailed discussion of a number of case histories in the file, the one tactic that was used most often—particularly with people in influential positions—was to offer

them high-paid jobs in government departments. They had pretty much determined that, where money was concerned, people usually comply.

But, there was a discussion of the so-called Men in Black—people going around warning people about national security and intimidating them into silence. However, Robert told us that this tactic was only used on those whose instability was considered to be significant enough that, if they ever told their story publicly, it would not be considered credible (Ibid.).

For all that, and if all else failed, Randles added to me, there was one final option: "termination" (Ibid.). Robert quietly told Randles that although, according to the files, this tactic wasn't employed too frequently, those that were charged with carrying out such assassinations were well trained to ensure that any "UFO-related deaths" appeared to be due to suicide or accident (Ibid.).

There is something else, too: Wright-Patterson Air Force Base, from where the seemingly classified files originated, played a significant role in the development of President Reagan's SDI program. When Reagan announced his "Star Wars" vision, one of the first official bodies tasked with researching the feasibility of SDI becoming a reality was the Air Force Office of Scientific Research (OSR), the origins of which date back to 1951. Critical to the research was a sub-project of OSR that operated out of Wright-Patterson, one whose SDI-themed work revolved around ultra-high-speed computing, laser technology, outerspace propulsion systems, and advanced sensor-based equipment. Is it only a coincidence that Wright-Patterson was home to highly classified files on UFOs, SDI-based work, and documents detailing murders made to look like suicide or accident? And was it only a coincidence that Jenny Randles was alerted to all of the above at the same time those SDI-Marconi deaths in the UK reached fever-pitch level?

Marconi Continues to be a Deadly Company to Work for

Not long after Dr. John Brittan died, around Christmas 1986, there was the very strange affair of Avtar Singh-Gida. He worked on classified programs for the British Ministry of Defense with ties to Marconi, and curiously went missing from Loughborough, England, on January 8, 1987. A full-scale manhunt was launched to find Singh-Gida. Fortunately, he turned up alive and well, albeit very confused—not surprising, as he finally surfaced, four months later, in Paris, France, unable to account for how or why he came to be there. It was almost as if someone—or *something*—had taken control of Singh-Gida's mental faculties and dictated his every move and action.

It was the matter of Singh-Gida's vanishing act, and the deaths of Vimal Bhagvangi Dajibhai and Arshad Sharif, that led John Cartwright—at the time the defense spokesman for the Liberal-Social Democratic alliance—to state that, as far as the deaths were concerned, and given the sensitive nature of the work on which the now-dead personnel were working, things had gone far beyond mere coincidence. Cartwright received a somewhat-predictable response from Lord Trefgarne, the government's Defense Procurement Minister, who conceded that although there was a small degree of oddness to the affair, an official investigation was not warranted. In fact, and in very intriguing words, Trefgarne added that not only was an inquiry unwarranted, it was also considered undesirable. But, undesirable to whom exactly, was never made clear.

It's also notable that in the very same year that Cartwright raised his concerns, the British *Observer* newspaper reported that the United States was then significantly emphasizing the need to protect those computer programmers employed on the SDI project. How intriguing that the United States was expressing concern about the safety of computer programmers with SDI links, when such people were dying left, right, and center in the UK. Someone in America's official infrastructure, it seems, was already exhibiting unease about the Marconi situation on the other side of the pond.

During the time period that Singh-Gida was missing, the life of a man named David Sands came to a violent end. Sands's employment was with a company called Elliott Automation Space and Advanced Military Systems Ltd., or EASAMS. On March 30, 1987, Sands inexplicably drove his car at high speed into a closed-down café on an exit road of the A33 highway. That Sands had placed two containers of gasoline in the trunk of his car ensured his death was both terrible and fiery.

A little more than a month later, one Michael Baker was also dead as a result of a car accident. Baker was an employee of Plessey, a company that, in 1999, was absorbed into BAE Systems when British Aerospace merged with Marconi Electronic Systems. While driving with friends on May 3, 1987, Baker seemingly lost control of his car on a clear stretch of English road. The car careered across the highway and flipped over. Fortunately, Baker's friends both survived. He, however, did not. Death was reportedly due to violent trauma to Baker's brain. His friends chose never to speak out publicly on the circumstances surrounding the crash.

On March 25, 1988, Trevor Knight, an engineer with Marconi, apparently killed himself by locking himself in his garage, attaching a hosepipe to the exhaust of his car, and dying from the fatal effects of carbon monoxide. Knight's family was baffled by his death, given that he had never displayed any evidence of having suicidal tendencies. Brigadier Peter Ferry, also of Marconi, committed suicide in the summer of 1988, as did Alistair Beckham, an employee of the aforementioned Plessey. Both men electrocuted themselves. Wholly outrageously, and also in 1988, the British Ministry of Defense claimed that the growing public interest in the ever-increasing list of deaths was due to nothing more than media sensationalism.

Then, in the latter part of 1991, the body of a Marconi employee named Malcolm Puddy was found floating in the waters of an English canal—only days after he told work colleagues he had uncovered something incredible that he wished to share with his bosses. What, exactly, Puddy stumbled upon, and why it was so incredible, remains unknown— to those outside of Marconi's highest echelons.

The deaths detailed here are merely the proverbial tip of the iceberg when it comes to the matter of the Marconi affair. To date, the number of British citizens with ties to Marconi who ended up dead under questionable circumstances between 1982 and 1991 is in excess of 30. For officialdom, suicides, accidents, and natural causes were the only answers. Not everyone was in accord with that unswerving stance, however.

When the Djinn Strikes

One of those who saw a direct connection between the deaths of the Marconi personnel and the UFO phenomenon was Gordon Creighton, a diplomat, an intelligence officer, and the editor of *Flying Saucer Review* magazine. In 1989, I interviewed Creighton about the flurry of Marconi deaths that the mainstream British media had already widely picked up on. Interestingly, Creighton's opinion was twofold.

First, Creighton felt that though at least *some* of the suicides and accidents were exactly that, the victims were driven to kill themselves via what Creighton termed a form of mind control. That's to say, chemical cocktails and "directed energy" weapons—perhaps not unlike those that may have been used on Morris K. Jessup decades earlier—were utilized to adversely manipulate the personalities of the victims, placing them into hypnotic-style states of depression and anxiety that allowed the minions of government to kill them as they saw fit (Redfern, 1989).

Then there was the second angle. Creighton suggested to me that, never mind the government, there was a concerted, worldwide effort on the part of an unearthly alien menace to try to ensure that the Strategic Defense Initiative never got off the ground, too. And the best way to do that was by killing those who were working on the program. Rather interestingly, Creighton did not believe the UFO phenomenon had extraterrestrial origins. Instead, he suspected the entities behind the phenomenon were nothing less than Djinn. Definitively paranormal in nature, Djinn are key entities within the lore and teachings of Islam that appear repeatedly in the *Qur'an* and that inhabit a world very different to ours—one of a different dimension, it might be suggested. The Djinn are not our friends. Quite the opposite: They are driven to provoke havoc, mayhem, and death for the human race, something they are extremely adept at doing.

One can understand why hostile, paranormal entities might want to have seen SDI shut down, but why would elements of British Intelligence follow a similar path? According to Creighton, there were certain figures within the British government who felt the wisest course of action was not to try to defeat the Djinn armada with President Reagan's SDI program, but to form a truce—granted, an admittedly uneasy one—with the visitors from beyond the veil. It was, claimed Creighton, a truce that would see certain world governments turn a blind eye to such things as alien abductions and Djinn-driven cattle mutilations. In return, the nightmarish creatures would hold off from a planetary takeover. They had one proviso, however: SDI had to go. In this scenario, said Creighton, agents of British intelligence were responsible for the killings of some of the Marconi people—specifically to try to accord with the wishes of the Djinn that the "Star Wars" project, and its staff, should not be allowed to proceed with their work (Ibid.).

Is it possible that in the United Kingdom highly classified research was undertaken in the 1980s and 1990s to kill people via highly advanced mind-control phenomena? If so, might those killings have been achieved by supernaturally rendering the victims into significantly altered states of deep depression and moroseness—states designed to push them down roads filled with engineered car accidents and suicides?

Certainly, when we look at the deaths of many of the Marconi scientists, we see repeated examples of sudden and decidedly out of character behavior, such as that exhibited by Avtar Singh-Gida, who fortunately avoided death but found himself wandering around Paris, France, in a definitive daze in May 1987; Michael Baker, whose death, also in May 1987, was caused by head trauma; and Malcolm Puddy's 1991 death in the depths of a British canal.

Were the numerous and varied deaths of the dozens of Marconi personnel—many with links to President Ronald Reagan's Strategic Defense Initiative—really the result of the combined efforts of both government agents and Djinn, one perhaps using regular tools of assassination and the other employing amazing, unearthly mind powers? As incredible as it may sound, and to paraphrase *The X-Files*, the threads of the story are out there. We may not, however, like where those same threads ultimately lead.

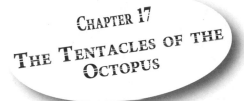

CHAPTER 17
THE TENTACLES OF THE OCTOPUS

Death in the Night

At first glance, it appeared to be nothing stranger than a tragic suicide—a man found dead in the bathtub of room 517 of the Sheraton Inn in Martinsburg, West Virginia, with significant slashes to his wrists. He left a poignant note, begging his loved ones to forgive him for his actions. A used wine glass gave a good indication of how the man spent his final few hours. His name was Danny Casolaro; he breathed his last breath on the night of August 9, 1991. There was, however, something about this particular, alleged suicide that suggested there was more to it than simply the actions of a desperately depressed man. At the time of his death, Casolaro, a 44-year-old freelance journalist and author, was hot on the trail of a well-hidden, powerful group of people. And, by all accounts, they were not to be messed with. That is, unless one had a warped yearning to end up prematurely dead, which, as circumstances dictated, was Casolaro's ultimate and exact fate.

About 18 months before his death, Casolaro was on the lookout for something fresh and exciting—something that would test his investigative skills to the max. To his joy—but also to his cost—Casolaro found it. It all began with a company called Inslaw, which was owned by a former employee of the National Security Agency, William Hamilton. As an expert in computer software, Hamilton created a program, called PROMIS, for the U.S. Department of Justice (DoJ) that was designed to significantly aid in the tracking of criminals. The only problem was that the DoJ accused Hamilton of inflating his fees for creating his program and quickly cancelled payments. A long and protracted legal battle ensued—one that Hamilton failed to win.

As Casolaro began to dig ever deeper into the story of Inslaw and PROMIS, he discovered that bootlegged versions of Hamilton's program were being peddled, by shadowy forces within the official infrastructure, to countless overseas nations, including Israel, Iran, and Iraq. There was a specific reason for this: The modified and bootlegged versions included an encrypted rear window that allowed U.S. Intelligence to effectively spy on just about any computer, or network, that utilized the PROMIS program. In that sense, Hamilton's creation was the perfect tool of espionage on America's enemies. But, what began for Casolaro as simply an investigation into a purloined computer program, the life of its irate creator, secret spying on overseas nations, and alleged DoJ chicanery, very soon became something else. Casolaro soon stumbled on, and possibly even incurred the deadly wrath of, something known as the Octopus.

UFOs and the Octopus

In his notes, Casolaro described the Octopus as an organization that, for more than 50 years, had manipulated on a truly massive scale. Governments, the oil industry, banking empires, and the dark world of organized crime were all at the mercy of the Octopus. The group, Casolaro discovered, played a significant role in not just the PROMIS scandal, but also in the molding of such historic events as the ill-fated Bay of Pigs affair of April 1961, the Cuban Missile Crisis of 1962, the Watergate scandal that brought down President Richard Nixon in 1974, and the horrific explosion of a packed Boeing 747 Jumbo Jet over Lockerbie, Scotland, in January 1988. But that was not all: The tentacles of the Octopus penetrated right into the fog-shrouded heart of the UFO mystery.

One aspect of Casolaro's work was focused on a project referred to as Yellow Lodge, supposedly a highly classified Octopus-sanctioned operation to develop and create new, exotic, and decidedly lethal viruses for use in warfare and assassination programs. According to Casolaro's sources, one of the secret installations where the nightmarish research was undertaken was buried deep below a northern New Mexico town called Dulce. Within UFO lore, Dulce has become infamous as the home of an alleged underground alien base, one controlled and run by hostile extraterrestrials. Casolaro, however, came to believe that the Octopus was responsible for spreading the alien-themed rumors, as part of an effort to deflect interest away from what was *really* afoot deep below the surface of Dulce— namely the development of advanced weaponry of the viral variety.

Casolaro's surviving files and notes also show that he spent time investigating the matter of the Majestic 12, allegedly a U.S. government group secretly created by President Harry S. Truman in 1947, following the notorious UFO crash at Roswell, New Mexico, that same year. Comprised of scientists, high-ranking military personnel, and members of the intelligence community, the Majestic 12—its proponents believe— were the keepers of the U.S. government's deepest and darkest secrets of the UFO kind. It must be stressed, however, that many UFO researchers conclude Majestic 12 to be nothing less than officially orchestrated disinformation.

With all that in mind, and given what Casolaro discovered about the duplicitous and manipulative situation in Dulce, New Mexico, it's not at all impossible that the Octopus may have played a role in the creation and dissemination of a Majestic 12–driven hoax. The purpose? To keep the UFO research community away from still-classified programs of a military (rather than alien) nature taking place in New Mexico in the late-1940s. Casolaro's papers also show that he was taking careful note of the UFO-themed stories coming out of the world's most well-known secret base, Area 51, as well as what was afoot at Pine Gap, Australia—whose staff work closely with the National Security Agency and from where numerous UFO reports have surfaced over the last 40 years or so.

Back to Maury Island

Most fascinating of all were Casolaro's connections to a man named Michael Riconosciuto, who claimed to have been one of the key players in the development of the so-called rear window in Inslaw's PROMIS program. But Riconosciuto was far more than just a hired hand in that particularly murky affair. It's a verifiable fact that in the 1950s Riconosciuto's father, Marshall, worked closely with none other than Fred Crisman, a man with links to both the deadly Maury Island UFO caper of June 1947 and the JFK assassination of November 22, 1963. Interestingly, Riconosciuto claimed that the craft seen over Maury Island—one of which seemingly exploded and rained large amounts of strange debris all over the waters of the Puget Sound harbor—were not alien spacecraft after all, but advanced, secret devices built and flown by Boeing, and powered by early, rudimentary nuclear reactors.

The data supplied by Riconosciuto, the material relative to the Majestic 12 controversy, and the information concerning what was afoot at Dulce, New Mexico, created in Casolaro's mind a scenario in which, since its very earliest years, the UFO subject had been brilliantly exploited to camouflage highly secret programs of a distinctly terrestrial nature—and the Octopus seemed to be deeply involved in that very same manipulation. Had his death not gotten in the way, it's very possible that Casolaro would have succeeded in exposing the shocking truth regarding how an entire UFO-themed mythos was created to protect the truth and secrecy surrounding futuristic aircraft and advanced weapons systems. But, unfortunately, death *did* get in the way.

Spiraling to the End

Very little is known about the final day, and the last hours, of Danny Casolaro's life. By all accounts, however, he was not a man on the verge of snuffing out his own existence. Rather, Casolaro seemed to be filled with vigor and was downright enthused by certain developments in his pursuit of the Octopus. For example, he eagerly shared—in the Sheraton Inn's bar—details of his Octopus-based research with the guest staying in the adjacent room. Similarly, less than 24 hours before his body was found, a jovial Casolaro met with a source in the aerospace industry, William Turner, and discussed with him the latest findings in the Octopus affair. As the two friends said their goodbyes, Casolaro made a joke about Turner watching his back. If only Casolaro had done likewise. We may never know for sure what happened over the course of the rest of August 9 and into August 10, except that whatever the cause of Danny Casolaro's death, the official verdict was that of suicide.

The Octopus Revisited

In 1996, a full-length book surfaced on the life, research, and controversial death of Danny Casolaro. Its title, unsurprisingly, was *The Octopus*. Its authors were Kenn Thomas and Jim Keith. Thomas was the editor of the conspiracy-based journal *Steamshovel Press* and someone who, three years later, penned *Maury Island UFO,* undeniably *the* definitive study of the death-filled events at Puget Sound (Tacoma, Washington) in June 1947— about which Danny Casolaro's source, Michael Riconosciuto, seemingly knew a great deal. Keith, meanwhile, was the author of a number of UFO-themed books, including *Casebook of the Men in Black, Black Helicopters Over America, Black Helicopters II,* and *Saucers of the Illuminati. The Octopus* very much picked up from where Casolaro's research came to a sudden, fatal, and irreversible halt in August 1991. Inspired and enthused by Casolaro's findings, Thomas and Keith pursued the Octopus, and its clandestine activities, with vigor and determination. In doing so, they, too, may have attracted attention of the distinctly deadly kind.

Death and Diana

Jim Keith was a man with many fingers in just about as many conspiratorial pies. In the summer of 1999, Keith was heavily involved in the investigation of a sensational story. It was one that suggested at the time of her controversy-filled death in August 1997, in Paris, France, that Diana, Princess of Wales, was pregnant by her lover, Dodi Fayed, a Muslim. The story was brought to Keith's attention by a powerful and influential disciple of Sufism, which is dedicated to the worship of Allah, the Arabic terminology for God. Keith's source made it clear that the British Royal Family, as well as the attendant, powerful British establishment, would simply not tolerate a half-Muslim child becoming a potential heir to the throne. The result: Diana had to be taken out of circulation—as in, permanently and quickly. And how did Keith's Deep Throat–style informant know all this? He had met with none other than Dodi Fayed's physician, who secretly and quietly revealed all. Keith, recognizing the potential enormity of the story, prepared an article on the revelations for the online outlet *Nitro News*. Keith planned on doing a follow-up article, too, in which the name of the doctor who not only claimed that Diana was pregnant, but who asserted he had personally confirmed the pregnancy, would be revealed. It was not to be, however. Something intervened in shocking fashion: Jim Keith's death.

Taking a Fall

In September 1999, Jim Keith headed out to the Burning Man festival, a yearly event held about 120 miles north of Reno, Nevada, in the Black Rock Desert. It's an incredibly popular celebration dedicated to "radical self-expression and radical self-reliance." The roots of Burning Man date back to the 1980s, when two men, Larry Harvey and Jerry James, set fire to an 8-foot-tall human effigy on a stretch of San Francisco's Baker Beach; the reason, chiefly, was to help Harvey put behind him the memories of a romance gone wrong. Since then, Burning Man has grown to huge and arguably epic proportions, with its themes ranging from evolution to fertility and the American Dream, and its attendance figures reaching close to 50,000. Even the fiery effigy itself has grown in stature—to a towering 50-foot-tall creation. Altered states, huge firework displays, and a celebration of all-things-alternative are the combined name of the game at Burning Man. The sacrificial aspect of the event—namely, the burning of a man-like figure—is something that was destined to take on a whole new meaning in the wake of Jim Keith's attendance (Burning Man..., 2013).

While chatting with like-minded friends and souls on one of the stages at Burning Man, Keith slipped and fell to the ground, a significant number of feet below. He just about managed to make his way back home, despite being in significant pain. By the following morning "significant" had been replaced by "overwhelmingly excruciating," to the point where

Keith had no choice but to call for an ambulance. He was quickly taken to Reno's Washoe Medical Center (today called Renown Health). X-rays determined that Keith had fractured his tibia, better known as the shin bone. The only available option was surgery. Having been advised by the attending doctor that a local anesthetic was utterly out of the question, Keith's paranoia began to grow, and perhaps justifiably so. Before he went under the knife, Keith told his nephew, Chris Davis, who had come along to the hospital to see how his uncle was doing, he feared if he was anesthetized he would never wake up. Incredibly, and tragically, that is *exactly* what happened.

The official story is that Keith's death—on the operating table, no less—was caused by a significantly sized blood clot that, having previously been lodged in Keith's lower leg, became loose and, upon reaching one of his lungs, killed him. The nature of the terrible event was quickly played down by the authorities. Anjeanette Damon, of the *Reno-Gazette Journal* newspaper, was told by the Washoe County deputy coroner that Keith's death was accidental and nothing else. But is that *really* all it was? It's very curious that Keith died at the exact same time he was planning to reveal what he was told concerning the 1997 death of Princess Diana. It's even more curious that for two weeks around the time of Keith's passing, the Website of *Nitro News*—the outlet due to publish Keith's never-written follow-up article—mysteriously crashed. Or it was *made* to crash.

Hacked to Pieces

There is another aspect of the complex and strange controversy surrounding the death of Jim Keith that is most assuredly worth mentioning and that may have a bearing on the online problems that plagued *Nitro News*. Between the last day of August 1999 and right up until just four days before Keith's untimely death, Keith corresponded via e-mail with Greg Bishop, a well-known and acclaimed author and investigator of many things weird, paranormal, and conspiratorial. Notably, the online conversations between Keith and Bishop revolved around how, near-simultaneously and in the immediate days just before Keith's passing, both men suffered severely at the hands of unknown computer hackers.

Keith e-mailed Bishop on August 31: "Last week I was hit with a virus, and all my personal files were wiped out" (Bishop, 2000). Though Keith was unsure as to whether or not this was indicative of the dark machinations of officialdom at work, he added: "I know a couple of other writers in this field who had the same thing happen to them at about the same time" (Ibid.).

In response, Bishop told Keith that only a few days before Keith's computer-based problems began, he (Bishop) powered up his computer and found, to his complete and utter consternation, that all of his articles and work-in-progress files had been systematically deleted. Fortunately, Bishop had taken the wise step of backing them up some time before. But, that was hardly the point. The most disturbing thing, from Bishop's perspective, was that the hacking had even occurred in the first place. As he informed Keith: "What was weird was the fact that the articles were not only 'trashed,' but were also deleted from the trash AND erased from the trash sector of the hard drive, making them unrecoverable," something that, as Bishop stressed, could not have been the result of mere error, because it took more than a few steps to successfully achieve (Ibid.). As to how such an action may have been performed, Bishop suggested to Keith that he was possibly hacked through his modem or, maybe, that he was "given a virus that only affects my article folder and no other Word files" (Ibid.). There was, however, a third possibility. It was a dark and disturbing possibility, one that caused Bishop some very understandable concern and a few, fraught, sleepless nights: Someone broke into Bishop's house and deleted the files.

Keith's final e-mail to Bishop, sent only four days before the former's death, read: "So far I've turned up nine political conspiracy sites that were hacked during the same time period" (Ibid.).

As for Bishop's thoughts on Keith's death, their e-mail exchange, and the unsettling spate of hacking that hit both men just before Keith died, he says: "I would prefer to think that there was no connection to the weird computer problems" (Ibid.). Whatever the truth of the curious and suspicious events that afflicted both Keith and Bishop, further death was looming on the horizon.

Biowarfare, Cattle Mutilations, and the Wicker Man

Ron Bonds was a close friend of Jim Keith, and the owner of IllumiNet Press, a company that published a number of Keith's UFO-based titles, including both *Saucers of the Illuminati* and *Casebook of the Men in Black*. Early on the morning of April 8, 2001, Bonds died from the effects of a severe attack of food poisoning that hit him late on the previous night. After Bonds's body was autopsied, a conclusion was reached that his death had been caused by exposure to *Clostridium perfringens,* one of the most common causes of food-borne illness. It might be justifiably said that the untimely deaths of Keith and Bonds (the former was 49 and the latter 48 at the times of their passing) were simply the results of tragic circumstances. On the other hand, maybe they weren't.

Rather astonishingly, Keith himself had actually written, in his final book for Bonds, *Biowarfare in America,* about certain toxins used by the military and the intelligence community that could make murder appear to be misfortune by creating huge blood clots in the lungs—which, ironically, just happened to be the very cause of Keith's own death. Moreover, one of Keith's particular interests was the cattle mutilation phenomenon. In an article for *Fate* magazine, Keith noted that a significant percentage of mutilated cattle had been deliberately injected with strains of clostridium bacteria, the specific kind of bacteria that abruptly ended the life of Ron Bonds. There is also the matter of Burning Man, itself, to consider.

There's absolutely no doubt that Burning Man has its parallels with an ancient Celtic festival, that of the torching of the Wicker Man. Records created by the Roman Empire between 58 BC and 50 BC reveal that the Celts had a deeply revered tradition of constructing huge, man-like figures out of wicker, a woven fiber used most recognizably in the creation of baskets. The purpose of the burning of the Wicker Man was to appease the gods of old and to ensure a bountiful, healthy, and prosperous new year. Interestingly, the Celts regularly sacrificed their own kind—by placing them inside the massive, wicker creations—and setting them on fire. Celtic lore taught that, above all else, the gods preferred an innocent soul, rather than one of a wrongdoer. Is it feasible that, in a strange and sinister fashion, Jim Keith's death served some unholy purpose, and that his death was orchestrated according to the teachings of an ancient, archaic order? Very possibly, yes.

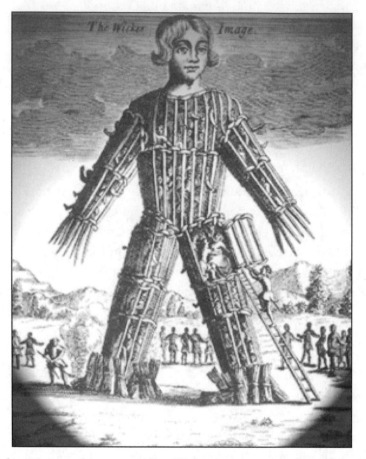

The Wicker Man: making a sacrifice (18th century, copyright unknown).

Curses, Hexes, and the CIA

In the late 1960s, the CIA quietly, and decidedly clandestinely, created a disturbing project codenamed Operation Often. It was a program designed to determine if certain paranormal phenomena had a viable place in the world of international espionage. The 20–30 personnel assigned to Operation Often spent their workdays focused upon a wide range of supernatural phenomena and tools, including Ouija boards, poltergeist activity, life after death, astrology, séances, and tarot cards. The staff of Operation Often also spent a great deal of time exploring an issue that may be relevant to the deaths of Danny Casolaro, Jim Keith, and Ron Bonds: curses.

Several members of the Operation Often team were tasked with determining if it was literally possible to create and direct onto a specific, targeted individual what most people would term "bad luck." Plans were initiated to harness and utilize supernatural phenomena to provoke ill health, terminal disease, and even death in certain presidents, prime ministers, and military figures of nations perceived as being potentially hostile to the United States. And attempts were made to create curses that would cause people to have fatal accidents, that would render individuals into suicidal states, and that would allow for what amounted to full-blown assassination, but without any telltale calling card of a physical nature ever left behind.

Could this have been what provoked the still-controversial deaths of Danny Casolaro, Jim Keith, and Ron Bonds? Just perhaps what appeared to be a suicide, an unfortunate fall from a stage, and a fatal dose of food poisoning—and which near-effortlessly forever took out of circulation three of the biggest names in the domain of 1990s-era UFO-themed or UFO-tinged conspiracy-theorizing—was something else entirely: assassination by malevolent hex.

And one final observation on this matter: Burning Man, where Jim Keith effectively met his end, was clearly inspired by the pagan, sacrificial rituals of the ancient Celts. It so transpires that the site on which Diana, Princess of Wales, met her death—the Paris, France Pont de l'Alma Tunnel—was, as far back as 500 AD, a place dedicated to the Moon goddess, Diana, and where sacrificial rites were routinely held. That Jim Keith was investigating the circumstances of Diana's death shortly before his very own demise—and that both he and the princess had links to places and events linked to human sacrifice—makes the possibility that the work of Operation Often and its possible successors worked not just well but fatally so. A final word of warning: keep away from octopuses. Their tentacles stretch a long way.

Chapter 18

A Killer Curse and a Deadly Date

The Wrath of Mothman

Mothman was a beast that dwelled in the eerie shadows of the West Virginian town of Point Pleasant from November 1966 to December 1967. Its macabre exploits were chronicled on screen in the 2002 hit Hollywood movie that starred Richard Gere, *The Mothman Prophecies*, named after the book of the same title written by paranormal investigator John Keel. A winged, humanoid-style entity, Mothman was most noted for its fiery red eyes, which struck cold fear into those that caught sight of them. At the time that Mothman dominated Point Pleasant, the town was also hit by a wave of encounters with alien entities, sightings of UFOs, run-ins with the nightmarish Men in Black, and a wide range of paranormal phenomena, such as poltergeist activity and the gift of prophecy. Things came to a crashing halt—quite literally a crashing halt—on December 15, 1967, when the town's Silver Bridge collapsed into the Ohio River, killing dozens in the calamitous process.

The Creature's Curse

It must be stressed that, because the Mothman encounters at Point Pleasant, West Virginia, occurred almost half a century ago, the inevitable passage of time has claimed the lives of more than a few players in the saga. Nevertheless, when we take a look at the catalogue of deaths that surround the activities of the weird winged thing, we do see an extraordinary number of fatalities that we might consider suspicious—particularly so because so many of them occurred in the wake of the release of the movie version of John Keel's book *The Mothman Prophecies.* Not only that, a number of those same fatalities involved people actually linked to the movie itself.

Both Jim Keith and Ron Bonds, who, as we have seen, died under questionable circumstances in relation to the so-called Octopus affair that also claimed the life of journalist Danny Casolaro, had connections to the Mothman enigma. Keith dug very deeply into the Point Pleasant events while researching the Men in Black controversy in the mid-1990s and came to a thought-provoking conclusion: Though he did not entirely rule out the possibility that genuine paranormal activity may have occurred in and around the town all those years ago, Keith felt that the most likely point of origin for the mystifying encounters was officialdom. In Keith's scenario, government agents, dressed in black, and using "drugs, flash guns, electronic harassment, electronic visual effects, and ultra-light aircraft simulating both UFOs and giant birds," were the likely cause of all the mayhem (Keith, 1997). As for Ron Bonds, in 1991, he republished John Keel's definitive study, *The Mothman Prophecies.* And Casolaro's place of death—Martinsburg, West Virginia—is only a four-hour trip by car to Point Pleasant.

On the very day that the movie version of *The Mothman Prophecies* was first aired in cinemas—January 25, 2002—Stephen Mallette, one of the first to have seen the flying fiend, was attending the funeral of his brother, Charlie, who passed on days earlier from the effects of a brain tumor. Over the course of the next week, five people were killed in car crashes in and around Point Pleasant. Less than two months later, the executive producer of *The Mothman Prophecies*, Ted Tannebaum, was dead from cancer. On the same day that the movie had its Australian premiere—May 23, 2002—a teenage boy of Fort Smith, Arkansas, named Aaron Stephen Rebsamen took his own life. He was the son of artist William Rebsamen, whose striking artwork adorns the cover of a book entitled *Mothman and Other Curious Encounters,* which was written by Mothman authority, Loren Coleman.

Then, on June 21, 2002, the body of a woman named Sherry Marie Yearsley was discovered near railroad tracks at Sparks, Nevada. A victim of murder, Yearsley was the former partner of none other than Ron Bonds. Six months later, a Mothman researcher, Susan Wilcox, was no more; a brain tumor that developed with astonishing speed took her life. Jessica Kaplan, a scenic artist on *The Mothman Prophecies* movie, was killed in a plane crash on June 6, 2003. Actor Alan Bates, who played the character Alexander Leek in the movie—a character based upon John Keel—died in the final days of December 2003. He was battling inoperable pancreatic cancer when a fatal stroke brought his life to an end. And, in July 2004, 42-year-old Jennifer Barrett-Pellington passed away in California. She was the wife of Mark Pellington, the director of *The Mothman Prophecies.*

A case can, of course, be made that when one goes looking for threads and deaths one can find them in any field of research, providing one digs deep enough. Maybe so, but, on the other hand, the sheer number of fatalities, and in such a clearly delineated period of time, does at the very least suggest becoming embroiled in the Mothman story may not be the wisest thing one could do with one's life.

June 24: The Worst Day of All—If You Are Into UFOs

Because this book began with the June 24, 1947, UFO encounter of Kenneth Arnold, it's only fitting that we close with June 24, too, and for one very good reason, as will now become apparent: In 1971, UFO investigator Otto Binder well and truly set a cat or several among the pigeons when he revealed the results of his inquiries into numerous mysterious deaths in Ufology. They were Binder's revelations that led many within the field of UFO research to take seriously the possibility that a dark and sinister force really was hard at work silencing flying saucer enthusiasts. One of the weirdest things that Binder discovered during the course of his studies was the wealth of UFO-related deaths that occurred on June 24—which, of course, just happened to be the date of Kenneth Arnold's famous UFO encounter over the Cascade Mountains, in Washington State, in 1947.

Back in 1950, Frank Scully, an American author and journalist, wrote a book titled *Behind the Flying Saucers.* The book was the very first title to deal with the emotive topic of crashed UFOs and alien bodies allegedly held by elements of the U.S. military. Although Scully did not reference the Roswell, New Mexico, event of 1947 in his book, he did cite other New Mexico–based crashed UFO incidents—something that, as the Freedom of Information Act has shown, led Scully and his informants to be watched very closely by the FBI. Scully passed away on June 24, 1964.

As we have already seen, none other than Edward Bryant, the central figure in the Scoriton affair of 1965, died on June 24, 1967. Bryant's case was hardly an isolated one. A young and promising researcher named Richard Church died suddenly, and from undermined causes, on June 24, 1967, too. Notably, at the time of his death, Church was looking into the links between the UFO phenomenon and the CIA, and had submitted a book proposal on that very subject to Bantam Books, which, at the time of Church's death, was just about to publish the paperback edition of researcher Frank Edwards's book *Flying Saucers—Here and Now!*

And on the matter of Frank Edwards...

The author of many books on the world of unexplained phenomena, including *Flying Saucers—Serious Business, Stranger Than Science* and *Strangest of All*, Frank Edwards was scheduled to speak at the World UFO Convention in New York on the very same day that both Edward Bryant and Richard Church died. Unfortunately, Edwards was unable to deliver his lecture—or, indeed, any lecture, ever again. He died of a heart attack only hours before the event began. The conference organizer, Jim Moseley, broke the news to the shocked audience.

Edwards's death was the result of a fatal heart attack, at age 59. Of course, he may simply have been unlucky to die at such a young age. The story, however, is not quite over. A well-known researcher of that era, Gray Barker—whose 1970 book, *The Silver Bridge,* chronicled the strange series of Mothman-connected deaths at Point Pleasant, West Virginia, in 1967—received several days in advance of the World UFO Convention a series of anonymous letters and phone calls warning him that Edwards would not survive the conference. That Edwards did not survive it makes the communications to Barker even more sinister. Shades of the fatal heart attacks of Captain Edward Ruppelt, of the U.S. Air Force's Project Blue Book in 1960, and remote-viewer Pat Price in 1975, perhaps?

And moving right along...

Although Erich Von Daniken is considered the heavyweight of the "Ancient Astronauts" controversy, before he came along there was someone else championing the theory that extraterrestrials visited the Earth thousands of years ago and may have deeply influenced humankind's legends, mythologies, and religions. That someone else was a Frenchman named Robert Charroux. His books included *Legacy of the Gods, Forgotten Worlds, The Gods Unknown*, and *Masters of the World*. He left this world on June 24, 1978. And we're still not done.

Without doubt, one of the strangest of all UFO-themed stories revolves around the acclaimed comedian and actor Jackie Gleason, perhaps best known for his 1950s television show *The Honeymooners.* It is not widely known that Gleason had a major interest in UFOs. His huge library on the subject ran to thousands of books. He followed the subject very closely, frequently appearing on the *Long John Nebel Show* (very much the *Coast to Coast* of the 1950s–1970s) to comment on and discuss the many and varied mysteries surrounding the subject. Another little-known fact is that Gleason was very good friends with President Richard Nixon. And it's on the matter of Gleason, Nixon, and UFOs to which we must now turn.

Jackie Gleason, one of many UFO enthusiasts who died on June 24 (Koll James, 1942).

According to Gleason's second wife, Beverly McKittrick, at some point in 1974, Nixon secretly arranged for Gleason to visit Homestead Air Force Base, in Florida, to see the remains of a number of small, preserved alien bodies held in a secure part of the base. It was, said McKittrick, a visit that the president and the comedian took together. The fragments of the story that are in the public domain suggest the visit was made in early 1974, which makes sense as Nixon resigned on August 9 of that year, as a result of the Watergate affair. Supposedly, very late one night, after a day of Gleason golfing with the president, there was a knock at the door of Gleason's Florida home. It was Nixon, minus any security personnel, and all alone. As researcher Mack Maloney notes: "This was not so unusual; Nixon was famous for giving his Secret Service detail the slip" (Maloney, 2013). Nixon told a somewhat-puzzled Gleason that he wanted to show him something—surely an understatement of mammoth proportions. With Nixon at the wheel, they hit the road for Homestead (Ibid.).

As the commander in chief, Nixon had no trouble accessing the well-guarded base, including its inner sanctum, where, apparently, something incredible was held under tight security. Even at that point, Gleason was puzzled by what was afoot, as Nixon was still saying nothing. Just a few minutes later, however, Gleason would know the reason for the clandestine, nighttime excursion. Nixon motioned his golfing buddy toward five or six freezer-like containers held in that same inner sanctum, each of which had a clear, glass top. As Gleason peered in, with a high degree of trepidation, he was shocked to see a number of small, humanoid figures, with large eyes and gray-hued skin, preserved within. Looking aged and not in the best of conditions, they appeared to be something definitively otherworldly.

Although Gleason, a firm believer in the UFO issue and a noted authority on the subject, was pleased to get vindication that his beliefs and research were not in vain after all, actually seeing the eerie evidence up close and personal was too much for even Gleason to stomach. It wasn't long before Nixon and Gleason were back on the road; the journey back to Gleason's home was reportedly made in stone-cold silence. Aside from confiding in his wife, Beverly, Gleason told very few people of his experience—one that should have been exciting, but that turned out to be wholly horrific and fraught. It's ironic that Jackie Gleason, having had such a deep and extensive interest in UFOs, and maybe even having seen hard proof of the reality of the phenomenon, died in 1987 on June 24.

We could speculate endlessly on the matter of whether or not the many UFO-linked deaths that occurred on June 24 amount to mere coincidence or something more unsettling, but, instead, we will close with the words of Otto Binder: "Something must account for the high death rate among Ufologists. That 'something' may either be the secret machinations of the UFO hierarchy who decides which earth-people 'know too much about flying saucers,' or the planned removal of UFO crusaders who have done their job nobly. Take your choice..." (Binder, 1971).

Conclusions

Our journey into the controversial world of mysterious deaths in Ufology is now over, which means it's time to try to formulate some observations and conclusions about our catalog of countless fatalities. Those of a skeptical mind, and who are doubtful of the theory that immersing oneself in the UFO issue can lead to an early, tragic, or violent death, would likely say that first and foremost we are all people, and that fatalities happen to people all the time. They would be absolutely right. Every single day, people die from the results of sudden heart attacks, muggings, car accidents, and terminal illnesses. Indeed, one can find such deaths in any walk of life. Those are, after all, the hazards of being alive!

That said, there are very good reasons for believing that the cases addressed within these pages fall into a very different category—one where accidents are not quite what they seem, where heart attacks are induced, and where suicides are anything but. Let's go back to the beginning.

If the events of March 4, 1946, involving Brazilian João Prestes Filho happened as we are assured they did, then very little room is left for a conventional explanation. As for the Maury Island saga of June 1947, the death and near-death rate was impressively grim, to the extent that coincidence seems unlikely: two dead pilots; a pair of dead journalists; a near-fatal accident for legendary UFO spotter Kenneth Arnold; threats to the life of Harold Dahl from a proto–Man in Black; and, finally, the Dahl family's dog. Can all of that really have been down to coincidence and nothing else? From my perspective, no, it certainly cannot.

Then there is Roswell, New Mexico, July 1947: early deaths, lives plunged into depression, severe alcoholism, despair, and suicide—or *assumed* suicide—as a result of exposure to whatever it was that really happened on the Foster Ranch, all those decades ago. And let's not forget those curious outbreaks of disease in Lincoln County, home of the legendary incident that attracted the attention of both J. Edgar Hoover and the director of the CIA. As for Captain Thomas Mantell and his death while allegedly pursuing a UFO in 1948, in the skies of Kentucky, well, we know he chased something, and history has shown he didn't make it out of the chase alive.

Moving on, is it merely coincidence that both Secretary of Defense James Forrestal and MKULTRA player Frank Olson fell to their deaths from windows on high, at a time when the CIA was actually instructing its agents on how to commit murder, and make it look like suicide, in this very manner? I suggest no, it's *not* a coincidence.

And what are we to make of the November 1953 affair of Karl Hunrath and Wilbur Wilkinson? Not only did they vanish into oblivion, but just a couple of weeks later, no less than four U.S. airmen lost their lives only a short distance from where Hunrath lived—a man who loudly claimed to have in his possession alien-derived technology capable of destroying U.S. military aircraft. Clearly, there are parts of this story that followed Hunrath and Wilkinson to the other side, if that is where they really went.

Then there is Morris K. Jessup, from my perspective someone driven to take his own life, possibly as a result of him having been targeted with sophisticated mood- and mind-altering technologies.

Moving right on up into the 1960s, there is the UFO-dominated matter of the JFK assassination, which tells us one thing more than anything else: If powerful individuals were willing to have the president of the United States of America taken out of circulation for what he knew about the UFO controversy, the idea that the average Ufologist could lose his or her life, too, becomes more and more likely. As for Edward Bryant's 1967 death in England, after an encounter of the very close variety, this seems to have been due to the over-zealous and reckless actions of government personnel utilizing sophisticated mind-manipulating technologies, rather than a deliberate act. That hardly mattered to Bryant, however; malicious or mistake, he still ended up dead.

Into the 1970s, we see the beginnings of an entirely different trend: the apparent targeting of people working on sensitive and highly secret projects for the military and the intelligence community. I am talking here about the highly suspicious passing of remote-viewer Pat Price and the deaths of Marconi personnel in the UK, a program of termination reactivated in the 1980s in relation to President Ronald Reagan's "Star Wars" project. Rather disturbingly, the fact that many of the individuals unfortunately caught up in these sorry affairs appeared to have been subjected to highly advanced mind-control technologies, heart attack–inducing weaponry, and murders made to look like suicide, shows just how far certain people will go to keep a classified secret exactly that.

As for the 1978 death of Kenneth Edwards and that of Zigmund Adamski in 1980, though the probability is high that their deaths were UFO-connected, we do not know if this was due to deliberate acts on the part of the intelligences behind the UFO phenomenon or catastrophic mistakes. If, however, we accept the accounts of Gordon Creighton on the matters and goals of Djinn, then it would be very wise to avoid these menacing, cold-hearted killers at all costs.

One death that almost certainly was not planned for, and that can be categorized as a terrible error, was that of Betty Cash, who, as a result of crossing paths with a UFO and a veritable squadron of helicopters in Texas late one December 1980 night, had her life cut short by cancer. That Cash was exposed to something of deadly proportions as she walked toward the unknown craft—whether one of ours or one of theirs—is a scenario of more than likely proportions.

Then there is the *really* dark side of this story: human mutilations and deaths by alien viruses. If these issues have even a modicum of reality to them, and the evidence strongly suggests they do, then to say that the UFO phenomenon is one of life-threatening—and life-extinguishing—proportions is not in any doubt. We have also seen that sometimes death is not confirmed, but only presumed, because we lack a corpse or corpses. The case of the aforementioned Karl Hunrath and Wilbur Wilkinson is a perfect example, though certainly the most famous is that of Frederick Valentich in 1978. Dead, kidnapped, or a new life somewhere else—we just don't know.

What about Danny Casolaro, Ron Bonds, and Jim Keith in relation to the Octopus saga and its UFO links? All the evidence here suggests the work of hired assassins, possibly—and incredibly—mixed in with the deadly, occult techniques born out of the CIA's Operation Often. Still on the matter of the occult, we have those cases that seem to have almost paranormal overtones to them, such as the many and eerie deaths that surround the Mothman phenomenon, and more than a few deaths on the date on which the flying saucer phenomenon was born: June 24. I wish I could bring myself to believe these latter deaths were all down to bizarre coincidences and nothing else. Unfortunately, I cannot.

What all of the above tells us is that the reasons why countless people—all allied to the UFO phenomenon in one way or another, and dating back to the 1940s—have met their maker are many and varied. On occasion, when someone has gotten a little too close to the UFO truth for his or her own good, death has occurred at the hands of hired guns and agents of officialdom. In other cases, being in the wrong place at the wrong time can snuff out a life in an instant, or over the course of years when lingering illness develops and overwhelms as a result. And we should also not forget those examples where the intelligences behind the UFO phenomenon have exhibited what can only be described as malicious, deadly behavior, and while showing little or no regard for human life.

To UFO witnesses, investigators, abductees, researchers, and just about anyone and everyone thinking of immersing themselves in the world of the flying saucer, I say this: tread very carefully, lest you tread no more. *Ever.*

BIBLIOGRAPHY

[Author's note: All Website addresses were last reviewed for accuracy in January 2014.]

"1954 French UFO Humanoid Encounters." *www.ufosnw.com/sighting_ reports/older/1954french/1954french.htm*.

"1980 Cash Landrum UFO a Wasp II Test Craft?" *http://cyber-space-war. blogspot.com/2012/08/1980-cash-landrum-ufo-wasp-ii-test-craft. html*. August 10, 2012.

"25 Marconi Scientists, 1982–88." *http://projectcamelot.org/marconi.html*.

Adams, Ronald L., and Dr. R.A. Williams. "Biological Effects of Electromagnetic Radiation (Radiowaves and Microwaves) Eurasian Communist Countries." Defense Intelligence Agency, March 1976.

Adams, Tom. *The Choppers—and the Choppers* (Paris, Tex.: Project Stigma, 1991).

Adamski, George, and Desmond Leslie. *Flying Saucers Have Landed* (London: Werner Laurie, 1953).

Albarelli, Jr., H.P. *A Terrible Mistake: The Murder of Frank Olson and the CIA's Secret Cold War Experiments* (Walterville, Oreg.: Trine Day LLC, 2009).

"Alien Abduction Claims in Yorkshire." *www.bbc.co.uk/insideout/ yorkslincs/series2/ufo_alien_abduction_yorkshire_pennine_ sighting_adamski_mystery.shtml.* February 3, 2003.

"Animal Mutilation." *http://vault.fbi.gov/Animal%20Mutilation.*

"Annex C Fragment." *www.majesticdocuments.com/pdf/annexc_fragment. pdf.*

"The Assassination of Princess Diana." *http://thenewalexandrialibrary. com/diana.html.*

Auchmutey, Jim. "The Strange Death of Conspiracy Book Publisher Ron Bonds." *Atlanta Journal,* June 14, 2002.

Auerbach, Loyd. "A Farewell to Dr. Karlis Osis." *The Llewellyn Journal. www.llewellyn.com/journal/article/62.*

Australian Department of Transport. "Light Aircraft Overdue." *http:// recordsearch.naa.gov.au/scripts/Imagine.asp?B=11485989.* October 25, 1978.

"BAE Systems." *www.baesystems.com/home?_ afrLoop=1940082953108000.*

Baker, Vary Judyth. *Me & Lee: How I Came to Know, Love and Lose Lee Harvey Oswald* (Walterville, Oreg.: Trine Day LLC, 2010).

Barker, Gray. *The Strange Case of Dr. M.K. Jessup* (Clarksburg, W.V.: Saucerian Press, 1974).

Berlitz, Charles, and William L. Moore. *The Philadelphia Experiment* (London: Granada Publishing Ltd., 1980).

———. *The Roswell Incident* (London: Granada Publishing Ltd., 1981).

Binder, Otto O. "Liquidation of the UFO Researchers." *Saga,* May 1971.

"Bioterrorism Agents/Diseases (by Category)." *www.bt.cdc.gov/agent/ agentlist-category.asp.*

Bishop, Greg. "My Last Email Exchange With Jim Keith." *Wake Up Down There!* (Kempton, Ill.: Adventures Unlimited Press, 2000).

———. *Project Beta* (New York: Paraview-Pocket Books, 2005).

"Blackheath Barrow: Todmorden's Ancient Circle." *www.calderdale.gov. uk/leisure/localhistory/glimpse-past/archaeology/ancient-circle.html.*

"Blackheath Circle, Todmorden, West Yorkshire." *http://megalithix. wordpress.com/2010/11/19/blackheath-circle/.* November 19, 2010.

Bowart, Walter. *Operation Mind Control* (London: Fontana, 1978).

Bowen, Charles. *The Humanoids* (London: Futura Publications, Ltd., 1969).

Boyle, Captain John E., U.S. Air Force. Letter to Nick Redfern, September 30, 1988.

Bragalia, Anthony. "The Roswell Undertaker's Secret Revealed." *http://ufocon.blogspot.com/2008_12_21_archive.html.* December 26, 2008.

———. "Roswell Alcoholics: The Alien Anguish." *http://ufocon.blogspot.com/2010/03/roswell-alcoholics-alien-anguish-by.html.* March 14, 2010.

———. "The Children Who Bore Witness to Roswell: Their Tragic Stories Finally Revealed." *http://bragalia.blogspot.com/2012/03/children-who-bore-witness-to-roswell.html.* March 5, 2012.

Brookesmith, Peter, David Clarke, and Andy Roberts. "Policeman Probed: British Bobby Abducted by Aliens!" *www.forteantimes.com/features/fbi/4903/policeman_probed.html.* January 2011.

Brown, Nimue. "The Truth About Wicker Men." *http://druidlife.wordpress.com/2011/11/01/the-truth-about-wicker-men/.* November 1, 2011.

Bruni, Georgina. *You Can't Tell the People* (London: Macmillan, 2001).

Buckle, Eileen. *The Scoriton Mystery* (London: Neville Spearman, 1967).

"Burning Man: Frequently Asked Questions." *www.burningman.com/whatisburningman/about_burningman/faq_what_is.html.* 2013.

"Bush, Miriam." *http://thedemoniacal.blogspot.com/2010/07/bush-miriam.html.* July 2, 2010.

Cameron, Grant. "Reagan UFO Story." *www.presidentialufo.com/ronald-reagan/99-reagan-ufo-story.* August 2, 2009.

Cannon, Martin. "The Controllers: Roswell, Truth and Consequences, Part II." *www.redshift.com/~damason/lhreport/articles/roswell2.html.*

Carey, Thomas J., and Donald R. Schmitt. "Mack Brazel Reconsidered." *International UFO Reporter,* Winter 1999.

———. *Witness to Roswell* (Pompton Plains, N.J.: New Page Books, 2009).

Carpenter, Paul. "The Alan Godfrey Abduction." *www.weirdisland.co.uk/skies/ufos/the-alan-godfrey-abduction.html.* March 28, 2012.

Chapman, Robert. *UFO: Flying Saucers over Britain?* (London: Granada Publishing, Ltd., 1981).

Coleman, Loren. *Mothman and Other Curious Encounters* (New York: Paraview Press, 2002).

————. "The Mothman Death List." *www.lorencoleman.com/mothman_ death_list.html.* August 20, 2005.

————. "New Rash of Mothman-Linked Deaths." *www.cryptozoonews. com/new-mm-deaths/.* April 15, 2007.

————. "Mothman Deaths Keep Away No One." *www.cryptozoonews. com/good-bad-ugly/.* July 24, 2007.

————. "Mothman Deaths: The Good, the Bad, and the Ugly." *www. cryptozoonews.com/good-bad-ugly/.* May 13, 2008.

Collins, Tony. *Open Verdict: An Account of 25 Mysterious Deaths in the Defense Industry* (London: Sphere Books, Ltd., 1990).

Colvin, Andrew B. "Mothman: The Angel of Conspiracy." *Paranoia,* Issue 47, Spring 2008.

————. *The Mothman Shrieks* (Seattle, Wash.: Metadisc Books, 2012).

Cooper, Milton William. *Behold a Pale Horse* (Flagstaff, Ariz.: Light Technology Publishing, 1991).

Corso, Philip, and William Birnes. *The Day After Roswell* (New York: Simon & Schuster, 1997).

Covert, Norman. "A History of Fort Detrick, Maryland." *www.detrick. army.mil/cutting_edge/index.cfm.* October 2000.

Damon, Anjeanette. "Rumors Abound in Death of Conspiracy Theorist." *Reno Gazette-Journal,* September 28, 1999.

Dodd, Tony. "Flight to Destruction: The Strange Death of Pilot Thomas Mantell." *www.crowdedskies.com/tony_dodd_thomas_mantell. htm.*

Dolan, Richard. "JFK and Our Secret History." *www.afterdisclosure. com/2011/01/jfk-secrecy.html.* January 20, 2011.

————. "The Extremely Strange Abduction of Charles Hickson." *www. afterdisclosure.com/2011/09/charles-hickson-abduction.html.* September 15, 2011.

"Duggan, Laurence Hayden (1905–1948)." *www.documentstalk.com/wp/ duggan-laurence-Hayden.*

"Dulce Underground Base." *www.ufocasebook.com/dulce.html.*

Dupre, Deborah. "Military's Dumped Mustard Gas Closes Gulf of Mexico's Horn Island." *www.examiner.com/article/military-s-dumped-mustard-gas-closes-gulf-of-mexico-s-horn-island.* August 20, 2012.

Ecker, Don. "Apparent FBI Stonewall-Report of Human Mutilations." *UFO Magazine,* Volume 4, Number 3, July–August, 1989.

Ecker, Don. "The Human Mutilation Factor." *www.sott.net/article/194149-Don-Ecker-The-Human-Mutilation-Factor.* October 9, 2004.

"The Edwards Case." *www.davidicke.com/forum/showthread.php?t=179980.*

Eldritch, Tristan. "The Curious Tale of Jackie Gleason, Richard Nixon, and the Dead Aliens." *http://2012diaries.blogspot.com/2009/11/curious-tale-of-jackie-gleason-richard.html.* November 15, 2009.

"Ellingson Award." *www.asmaafg.org/html/ellingson_award.html.*

Evans, Hilary, and Robert Bartholomew. *Outbreak! The Encyclopedia of Extraordinary Social Behavior* (San Antonio, Tex.: Anomalist Books, 2009).

Fawcett, Lawrence, and Barry J. Greenwood. *Clear Intent: The Government Cover-Up of the UFO Experience* (Englewood Cliffs, N.J.: Prentice-Hall, Inc., 1984).

"FBI Drums Up Cymbals-Like 'Disk' in Idaho." *Tacoma News Tribune,* July 12, 1947.

Federal Bureau of Investigation. "Bacteriological Warfare in the United States." March 29, 1950.

———. "George Adamski." November 29, 1953.

Fogarty, John. "Human Mutilations III – The Idaho Hunter." *www.thegodkey.com/blog/2013/04/07/HUMAN-MUTILATIONS-III-THE-IDAHO-HUNTER.aspx.* April 7, 2013.

"Forrestal Is Treated in Naval Hospital for Nervous and Physical Exhaustion." *New York Times,* April 7, 1949.

"Forrestal Killed in 13-Story Leap; U.S. Mourning Set." *New York Times,* May 23, 1949.

"Forrestal's Suicide Leap Brings Inquiry by Navy." *Los Angeles Times,* May 23, 1949.

Fort, Charles. *The Book of the Damned* (New York: Cosimo Books, 2004).

Fricker, Richard L. "The Inslaw Octopus." *www.wired.com/wired/archive/1.01/inslaw_pr.html.* 2004.

Frommer, Frederic, J. "Frank Olson Family's Lawsuit Against Alleged CIA Murder Dismissed." *www.huffingtonpost.com/2013/07/17/frank-olson-lawsuit-dismissed_n_3611911.html.* July 17, 2013.

Fuller, John G. *The Interrupted Journey* (New York: Dial Press, 1966).

———. *The Day of St. Anthony's Fire* (London: Hutchinson, 1969).

———. *Incident at Exeter* (New York: Berkeley, 1971).

Garrison, Jim. *On the Trail of the Assassins* (London: Penguin, 1988).

Genzlinger, Anna Lykins. *The Jessup Dimension* (Clarksburg, W.V.: Saucerian Press, 1981).

"George Adamski." Federal Bureau of Investigation file. 1953. Declassified under the terms of the Freedom of Information Act.

Good, Timothy. *Above Top Secret* (London: Sidgwick & Jackson, 1987).

Halbritter, Ron. "The Hoax on You: Before the UFO Crash at Roswell, There Was...Maury Island." *Steamshovel Press,* Number 12, 1995.

Hall, Richard. "Kinross AFB/F-89 Disappearance: November 23, 1953." *www.nicap.org/reports/kinross.htm.* 2013.

Hanohano, Katiuska, and Kalani Hanohano. "Notorious Fred Crisman." *UFO Magazine,* Volume 9, Number 1, 1994.

Hansson, Lars. *UFOs, Aliens and "Ex"-Intelligence Agents: Who's Fooling Whom?* (Orlando, Fla.: Paragon Research and Publications, 1991).

Heath, Gord. "The Kinross Incident." 2014.

Hellier, Chris. "The Case of the Cursed Bread." *www.forteantimes.com/ strangedays/misc/3307/the_case_of_the_cursed_bread.html.* April, 2010.

Holdsworth, Nick. "Prime Suspect in Georgi Markov 'Umbrella Poison' Murder Tracked Down to Austria." *www.telegraph.co.uk/news/ uknews/crime/9949856/Prime-suspect-in-Georgi-Markov-umbrella- poison-murder-tracked-down-to-Austria.html.* March 23, 2013.

Hoopes, Townsend, and Douglas G. Brinkley. *The Life and Times of James Forrestal* (Annapolis, Md.: Bluejacket Books, 2000).

"Horn Island, MS." *http://uxoinfo.com/blogcfc/client/includes/uxopages/ sitedata1.cfm?uxoinfo_id=10MS0082.*

"Hospital Is Absolved by Mrs. Forrestal." *New York Times,* May 26, 1949.

Huff, Chris. "Cave Canem." *www.assap.ac.uk/newsite/Docs/Black%20 dogs.pdf.*

Ignatieff, Michael. "Who killed Frank Olson?" *www.theguardian.com/ books/2001/apr/07/books.guardianreview4.* April 6, 2001.

Jessup, Morris K. *The Case for the UFO* (New York: Citadel Press, 1955).

———. *The UFO Annual* (New York: Citadel Press, 1956).

———. *UFOs and the Bible* (New York: Citadel Press, 1956).

———. Letter to Manson J. Valentine, March 26, 1957.

———. *The Expanding Case for the UFO* (New York: Citadel Press, 1957).

"Jim Garrison: Interview With *Playboy* 5: Oswald and Banister in New Orleans." *http://22november1963.org.uk/jim-garrison-oswald-banister-new-orleans.*

"Jim Keith." *http://projectcamelot.org/keith.html.*

"Jim Keith Has Died!" *www.subgenius.com/updates/X0002_Jim_Keith_has_died.html.*

"Jim Keith—Sirius and the Illuminati." *http://mysteriesofsirius.com/sirius-researchers/jim-keith-1949-1999/.*

Jones, William, and Rebecca Minshall. *Bill Cooper and the Need for More Research* (Dublin, Ohio: MidOhio Research Associates, 1991).

Jura, Michael. "Remote Viewing—Was the Pat Price Experiment Successful?" *http://blog.learnremoteviewing.com/?p=38.*

Keel, John A. *The Mothman Prophecies* (New York: Tor, 1991).

Keith, Jim. *Black Helicopters Over America* (Lilburn, Ga.: IllumiNet Press, 1994).

———. *Black Helicopters II* (Lilburn, Ga.: IllumiNet Press, 1994).

———. *Casebook of the Men in Black* (Lilburn, Ga.: IllumiNet Press, 1997).

———. *Biowarfare in America* (Lilburn, Ga.: IllumiNet Press, 1999).

Keyhoe, Donald E. *Aliens From Space* (New York: New American Library, 1974).

Kilgallen, Dorothy. "Flying Saucer News." *Los Angeles Examiner,* May 23, 1955.

Kimery, Anthony. "The Secret Life of Fred L. Crisman." *UFO,* Volume 8, Number 5, 1993.

Kress, Dr. Kenneth A. "Parapsychology in Intelligence." *Studies in Intelligence,* Central Intelligence Agency, Winter 1977 issue.

Krystek, Lee. "The Mantell Incident." *www.unmuseum.org/mantell.htm.* 1998.

Lear, John. "Lear's Aliens." *www.bibliotecapleyades.net/vida_alien/esp_vida_alien_18o.htm.* December 29, 1987.

"Lee Harvey Oswald." *www.universityarchives.com/Find-an-Item/Results-List/Item-Detail.aspx?ItemID=57315.*

Lendman, Stephen. "MK-Ultra—The CIA's Mind Control Program." *http://rense.com/general89/mkultra.htm.* February 16, 2010.

Lewis, Neil A. "Reporter Is Buried Amid Questions Over His Pursuit of Conspiracy Idea." *New York Times,* August 17, 1991.

Lindseth, Shawn. "Awesome or Off-Putting: The Dead Marconi Scientists Mystery." *www.hecklerspray.com/awesome-or-off-putting-the-dead-marconi-scientists-mystery/20063399.php.* June 5, 2006.

MacMichael, David. "The Mysterious Death of Danny Casolaro." *http://salonesoterica.wordpress.com/2013/06/30/the-mysterious-death-of-danny-casolaro-by-david-macmichael-re-inslaw-case-at-american-buddha-online-library/.* June 30, 2013.

"Major General Theodore Cleveland Bedwell, Jr." *www.af.mil/information/bios/bio.asp?bioID=4642.*

Maloney, Mack. *Beyond Area 51* (New York: Berkley Books, 2013).

"Man Who Was 'Captured by UFOs With Grey Leathery Skin and Crab Claws' 40 Years Ago Reveals How it Changed His Life." *www.dailymail.co.uk/news/article-2454234/Man-captured-UFOs-crab-claws-1973-says-turned-life-upside-down.html.* October 11, 2013.

Marrs, Jim. *Crossfire: The Plot that Killed Kennedy* (New York: Carroll & Graf Publishers, 1989).

Marshall, Tyler. "Their Firm Linked to 'Star Wars': British Scientists' Deaths—Suicides or Conspiracy?" *Los Angeles Times,* April 8, 1987.

Martin, David. "Who Killed James Forrestal?" *www.dcdave.com/article4/021110.html.* November 10, 2002.

Mauso, Pablo Villarubia. "The Incredible Saga of João Prestes." *www.ufoinfo.com/news/joaoprestes.shtml.*

Milner, Terry. "The Very Strange Death of Top Remote Viewer Pat Price." *http://rense.com/general9/stranged.htm.* March 17, 2001.

Moore, William L. *The Philadelphia Experiment: Update* (Burbank, Calif.: William L. Moore Publications, 1984).

Morphy, Rob. "The Curse of the Silver Man." *http://mysteriousuniverse.org/2011/10/the-curse-of-the-silver-man/.* October 28, 2011.

———. "Death from Above – Part One: The Horrible Melting Man." *http://mysteriousuniverse.org/2012/06/death-from-above-part-one-the-horrible-melting-man/.* June 4, 2012.

Moseley, Jim. Notes, prepared in December 1953 by Moseley for a book that was never written. A copy of the relevant material is in the possession of Nick Redfern.

"Mutilation of Two Cows." Federal Bureau of Investigation document, October 14, 1976.

NASA. "John F. Kennedy Moon Speech—Rice Stadium, September 12 1962." *http://er.jsc.nasa.gov/seh/ricetalk.htm.*

"National Security Act Memorandum No. 271 Cooperation with the USSR on Outer Space Matters, 11/12/1963." *http://research. archives.gov/description/193642.*

"Nuclear Development in the United Kingdom." *www.world-nuclear. org/info/Country-Profiles/Countries-T-Z/Appendices/Nuclear-Development-in-the-United-Kingdom/.* January 2013.

"Observations of Traveler in USSR" Air Intelligence Information Report, October 14, 1955.

Oliver, Norman. *Sequel to Scoriton* (Self-published, 1968).

"Operation Often: Satanism in the CIA." *http://coverthistory.blogspot. com/2007/12/operation-often-satanism-in-cia-this.html.* December 17, 2007.

Padbury, Wendy. *The Plague Makers* (London: Vision Paperbacks, 2002).

Palmer, Raymond, and Kenneth Arnold. *The Coming of the Flying Saucers* (Amherst, Wisc.: 1952).

———. *The Coming of the Saucers* (London: Legend Press, 1996).

"Paraphsyics R&D—Warsaw Pact." U.S. Air Force, Foreign Technology Division, March 30, 1978.

Parry, Gareth. "Peace Women Fear Electronic Zapping at Base." *Guardian,* March 10, 1986.

"Pat Price." *www.remoteviewed.com/remote_viewing_patprice.htm.*

Perez, Robert C., and Edward F. Willett. *The Will to Win: A Biography of Ferdinand Eberstadt* (Santa Barbara, Calif.: Praeger, 1989).

"The Piney Woods Incident, Cash-Landrum." *www.ufocasebook.com/ Pineywoods.html.*

Ploeg, Dick Vander. "New Evidence: The Kinross UFO Incident." *http:// ufodigest.com/news/0806/kinross.html.* August 6, 2006.

"President/Founder." *www.ulchq.com/founder.htm.*

Puharich, Andrija. *The Sacred Mushroom: Key to the Door of Eternity* (New York: Doubleday, 1974).

Randle, Kevin D. "An Analysis of the Thomas Mantell UFO Case." *www.nicap.org/docs/mantell/analysis_mantell_randle.pdf.*

Randle, Kevin D., and Donald R. Schmitt. *UFO Crash at Roswell* (New York: Avon, 1991).

———. *The Truth About the UFO Crash at Roswell* (New York: M. Evans, 1994).

Randles, Jenny. *The Pennine UFO Mystery* (St. Albans, UK: Granada Publishing, Ltd., 1983).

———. *The UFO Conspiracy* (New York: Sterling Publishing Company Inc., 1988).

———. *From Out of the Blue* (New Brunswick, N.J.: Inner Light-Global Communications, 1991).

———. *Alien Contact: The First Fifty Years* (Darby, Penna.: Diane Publishing Company, 1997).

———. *UFO Crash Landing?* (London: Blandford, 1998).

Rayelan. "Strange Death of Jim Keith." *www.rumormillnews.com/cgi-bin/archive.cgi?read=20193.* June 9, 2002.

"Reagan's Extraterrestrial Fixation—Will Records Reveal UFO Fixation?" *www.examiner.com/article/reagan-s-extraterrestrial-fixation-will-records-reveal-ufo-briefing.* April 12, 2009.

Redfern, Nick. Interview with Gordon Creighton, May 29, 1989.

———. Interview with Nick Pope, January 22, 1997.

———. Interview with Jenny Randles, March 28, 1997.

———. Interview with William Holden, October 22, 1997.

———. Interview with Rita Hill, June 5, 1998.

———. "Marilyn and Roswell." *http://mysteriousuniverse.org/2011/09/marilyn-roswell/.* September 15, 2011.

———. "Kidnapped by a Flying Saucer?" *http://mysteriousuniverse.org/2012/04/kidnapped-by-a-flying-saucer/.* April 6, 2012.

———. *For Nobody's Eyes Only* (Pompton Plains, N.J.: New Page Books, 2013).

———. "Gunning for Answers." *Penthouse,* December 2013.

Reitzes, David. "The JFK 100: Who Was Guy Banister?" *www.jfk-online.com/jfk100whoban.html.* 2001.

Report of the President's Commission on the Assassination of President Kennedy (Washington, D.C.: United States Government Printing Office, 1964).

Report of the Select Committee on Assassinations of the U.S. House of Representatives (Washington, D.C.: United States Government Printing Office, 1979).

"Research Findings on the Chihuahua Disk Crash" March 23, 1992.

Reynolds, Rich. "The Villas Boas Event." *http://ufor.blogspot.com/2006/01/villa-boas-event.html.* January 11, 2006.

Rifat, Tim. *Remote Viewing: What it Is, Who Uses it, and How to Do It* (London: Vision Paperbacks, 2001).

Ritter, Ted. "Mysterious Deaths, Freedom of Information, Marconi and the Ministry of Defense." *www.computerweekly.com/blogs/public-sector/2006/11/mysterious-deaths-freedom-of-i.html.* November 29, 2006.

Robbins, Peter. "The Strange Death of James Forrestal." 1st UFO Crash Retrieval Conference Proceedings (Broomfield, Colo.: Wood & Wood Enterprises, 2003).

Robinson, Ben. *The MagiCIAn: John Mulholland's Secret Life* (Somerville, Mass.: Lybrary.com, 2008).

Rojas, Alejandro. "Jackie Gleason Says Nixon Showed Him ETs." *www.openminds.tv/gleason-ets/5978.* October 12, 2010.

"Ron Bonds." *http://projectcamelot.org/bonds.html.*

Ruppelt, Edward J. *The Report on Unidentified Flying Objects* (New York: Ace Books, 1956).

Samuel, Henry. "French Bread Spiked With LSD in CIA Experiment." *www.telegraph.co.uk/news/worldnews/europe/france/7415082/French-bread-spiked-with-LSD-in-CIA-experiment.html.* March 11, 2010.

Sanchez, Raf. "Scientist Frank Olson Was Drugged With LSD and 'Murdered by CIA.'" *www.telegraph.co.uk/news/worldnews/northamerica/usa/9710121/Scientist-Frank-Olson-was-drugged-with-LSD-and-murdered-by-CIA.html.* November 28, 2012.

"Saucer Investigators in Strange Disappearance." *Los Angeles Mirror,* November 20, 1953.

Schnabel, Jim. *Remote Viewers: The Secret History of America's Psychic Spies* (New York: Dell, Publishing, 1997).

Schuessler, John F. *The Cash-Landrum UFO Incident* (Geo-Graphics, 1998).

Schulgen, Brigadier General George. "AMC Opinion Concerning 'Flying Discs.'" *www.project1947.com/fig/twinng47.htm.* 1947.

"Scorriton." *www.visitsouthdevon.co.uk/explore-south-devon/scorriton-p435763map.*

Scott, Irena, and William E. Jones. "The 'Unspeakables': Human Mutilations and Missing Children." *www.mufonohio.com/mufono/humutes.html.*

Scully, Frank. *Behind the Flying Saucers* (New York: Henry Holt & Company, 1950).

"Second Truax Jet, 2 Fliers Missing." *Capital Times,* November 24, 1953.

Senate Select Committee on Intelligence. "The Senate MK-Ultra Hearings." Washington, D.C., August 3, 1977.

Shachtman, Noah. "CIA's Lost Magic Manual Resurfaces." *www.wired. com/dangerroom/2009/11/cias-lost-magic-manual-resurfaces/.* November 24, 2009.

"Shades of Buck Rogers! This Is What Landed in Twin Falls." *Twin Fall Times,* July 11, 1947.

Simkin, John. "Guy Banister." *www.spartacus.schoolnet.co.uk/ JFKbannister.htm.*

Simkin, John. "Sidney Gottlieb." *www.spartacus.schoolnet.co.uk/ JFKgottlieb.htm.*

Simpson, Cornell. *The Death of James Forrestal* (Boston, Mass.: Western Islands, 1966).

Sparks, Brad. "FBI Interrogates UFO Researcher: Government May Confiscate Documents." *APRO Bulletin*, Volume 27, Number 1, July 1978.

Special Branch. "Unidentified Aircraft—Marconi, New Street, Chelmsford, May 12, 1973." May 14, 1973.

Stacy, Dennis. "Forrestal's Fall: Did He Jump, or Was He Pushed?" *Flying Saucer Review,* Volume 38, Number 9, 1993.

Steiger, Brad, Sherry Steiger, and Al Bielek. *The Philadelphia Experiment and Other UFO Conspiracies* (New Brunswick, N.J.: Inner Light, 1990).

Strainic, Michael. "James Wilbert B. Smith (1909–1961). Brief Biography." *www.nicap.org/bios/wbsmith.htm.*

"The Strange Death of Zigmund Adamski." *http://sjhstrangetales. wordpress.com/2012/02/16/the-strange-death-of-zigmund-adamski/.* February 16, 2012.

"The Strategic Defense Initiative (SDI): Star Wars." *www.coldwar.org/ articles/80s/SDI-StarWars.asp.*

Stringfield, Leonard. "Mantell's Last Word." *CRIFO Newsletter,* 1954.

———. *Situation Red: The UFO Siege* (London: Sphere Books Ltd., 1978).

———. *UFO Crash/Retrievals: The Inner Sanctum* (Cincinnati, Ohio: Published privately, July 1991).

"A Study of Assassination." *www2.gwu.edu/~nsarchiv/NSAEBB/ NSAEBB4/docs/doc02.pdf.* 1951.

Thomas, Gordon. *Journey Into Madness* (London: Corgi, 1988).

Thomas, Kenn. *Maury Island UFO* (Lilburn, Ga.: IllumiNet Press, 1999).

———. "Casolaro's Octopus." *www.theforbiddenknowledge.com/ hardtruth/casolaro_octopus.htm.* June 7, 2001.

Thomas, Kenn, and Jim Keith. *The Octopus: Secret Government and the Death of Danny Casolaro* (Los Angeles, Calif.: Feral House, 1999).

———. *The Octopus: Secret Government and the Death of Danny Casolaro, Revised Edition* (Los Angeles, Calif.: Feral House, 2004).

Thomson, Mike. "Pont-Saint-Esprit Poisoning: Did the CIA spread LSD?" *www.bbc.co.uk/news/world-10996838.* August 23, 2010.

"Todmorden 'UFO Alley.'" *www.ourufosociety.com/ufo-news-articles/ todmorden-ufo-alley/.* January 16, 2011.

Torres, Noe, and Ruben Uriarte. *Mexico's Roswell: The Chihuahua UFO Crash* (College Station, Tex.: VBW Publishing, 2007).

"Trips: Brooks Air Force Base, Texas, 21 November 1963." *www. jfklibrary.org/Asset-Viewer/Archives/JFKPOF-109-011.aspx.*

Trubshaw, Bob. *Explore Phantom Black Dogs* (Marlborough, UK: Heart of Albion Press, 2005).

"What if Pat Price Were Here?" *http://hereticalnotions.com/2010/12/13/ what-if-pat-price-were-here/.* December 13, 2010.

"Who Killed Off Star Wars Scientists?" *www.ufoevidence.org/documents/ doc826.htm.*

Williamson, George Hunt. *Other Tongues, Other Flesh* (Self-published, 1953).

Wood, Dr. Robert M., and Ryan S. Wood. *The Majestic Documents* (Redwood City, Calif.: Wood & Wood Enterprises, 1998).

"Working on the Suicide Squad: At Risley Royal Ordnance Factory." *www.bbc.co.uk/history/ww2peopleswar/stories/07/a2311507.shtml.* February 18, 2004.

INDEX

ABOUT NICK REDFERN

NICK REDFERN works full-time as an author, lecturer, and journalist. He writes about a wide range of unsolved mysteries, including Bigfoot, UFOs, the Loch Ness Monster, alien encounters, and government conspiracies. His previous books include For Nobody's Eyes Only, Monster Files, The World's Weirdest Places, The Pyramids and the Pentagon, Keep Out!, The Real Men in Black, The NASA Conspiracies, Contactees, and Memoirs of a Monster Hunter. He writes for MUFON UFO Journal and Mysterious Universe. Nick has appeared on numerous television shows, including Fox News; the History Channel's Ancient Aliens, Monster Quest, and UFO Hunters; VH1's Legend Hunters; National Geographic Channel's The Truth about UFOs and Paranatural; BBC's Out of this World; MSNBC's Countdown; and SyFy Channel's Proof Positive. He can be contacted at http://nickredfernfortean.blogspot.com.